The Not So Great America

Gemechu Birehanu Bekana

Published by Geme, 2023.

While every precaution has been taken in the preparation of this book, the publisher assumes no responsibility for errors or omissions, or for damages resulting from the use of the information contained herein.

THE NOT SO GREAT AMERICA

First edition. November 30, 2023.

ISBN: 979-8223785828

Written by Gemechu Birehanu Bekana.

Table of Contents

This book is dedicated to Americans and all the mediums that introduced me to the Great nation of America starting from Hollywood to News and everything. I also especially want to dedicate this book to the two lovely ladies from San Diego Caiifornia who came to my small town to teach English and left a lasting impact on my life.

Chapter one: America the Mythical land

"Let your mind start a journey through a strange new world. Leave all thoughts of the world you knew before. Let your soul take you where you long to be...Close your eyes let your spirit start to soar, and you'll live as you've never lived before." Erich Fromm

BEFORE I KNEW EGYPT or Greece or Rome and their ancient civilization in history classes, or before I knew any fancy nation to rave about there was only one nation that I know as mythical as the Greeks or as legendary as the Romans or as famous as the Egyptians or as fancy and flashy as the Emiratis of Dubai; apart from my birth nation Ethiopia and that mythological nation is none other than the United States of America that is located 10,000 Kilometers away from where I am.

The United States of America is may be the second country I know in my early childhood. It is not like I haven't studied the East African neighboring nations in my early classes on maps, but I really did not understand what they mean at all, for me they were just a bunch of shapes surrounding Ethiopia. And no one can blame it on me since I never heard someone talk about those neighboring nations except Eretria which used to be part of Ethiopia once. That is maybe why I have Ethiopia and one more great country in the whole world in my mind since I was a little kid.

As kids in school or village playgrounds (that is to refer to just a plain of grass or mud free to run and play around and not to be confused with real playgrounds you might think of) we used to talk a lot about a country that is legendary and mythological than that of ours or any country in the whole world for that matter.

That is a powerful nation that can easily dissipate or destroy anybody within a fraction of a second. That is an intelligent country that knows every move of everyone in the entire world. A nation that is clearly watching all of human kind and the planet from above (Don't ask me where we thought that was at that early childhood age; no one knows whether it was the moon or some satellite we just assumed it is from up there)

The Unite States of America in our little, totally misinformed and pure mind is the only largest, richest, majestic, powerful, influential and irresistible country in the whole world.

Despite all our resource limitations and miserable looking livelihood in a third world country as little kids in a remote village in Eastern Africa, we were always curious about what lies beyond the sky like may be every other kid on the planet. And may be unlike the other kids from the planet anyone in our group could agree the fact that only God and America know what lies beyond the sky.

These incredible views about the United States of America are not really transcribed from books, movies, or Schools at that exact time of my childhood to be specific. Because, during this period the only access to the outside world I know in my small town was a BBC radio program in English transmitted from London in the United Kingdom which my dad used to listen to. Unfortunately, I was not capable of hearing what it is because I was still not familiar with the English language at all. So, all our views about America are very original and authentic to us kids that is never heard anywhere else maybe. Not even America has that amazing and elaborate view about itself.

All the kids of the group in our small communal village have different stories they have heard about America being this great nation from family members and others that might have come into contact with some one who went to America and we all kids improvise those stories in a manner that should make our stories stand out from the rest of the kids. That created a whole new story that has never been heard anywhere else just true to us in that small rural village of Eastern Ethiopia.

We created, scripted, narrated and told an entirely surreal and dream like stories about the United States of America amongst ourselves just to be the kid with coolest story. Even though these stories are all made up they have been instrumental in shaping our views about the nation of America in general in the rest of our lives.

One of such surreal stories involve a tale of milk being delivered through the tap to every household living in America which we used to believe firmly and heard it in aw at the time. I remember being smitten by this story and also trying to create my own version of another story to outshine among the group with my incredible story about the United States. I might not really remember which stories were created by me exclusively or co created with my fellow enthusiasts but I can recall a bunch of absurd and great stories

Stories like an American soldier destroying an enemy anywhere without a single casualty; stories like teachers and soldiers being the highest paid employees in the US (This an issue because in my country these two professions are the least paid employees down the line of civil servants so we use to hail the mythological nation of US where people who we really admire the most as a child are paid the highest amount of money). To my surprise or despair just like Ethiopia I later found out this two people or professionals are not paid well enough in the US too.

Our collective stories in those ages of innocence, foolishness and pure stupidity are a contrasting indication of America where there is no sickness, no worries, no poor, America that has petroleum products delivered home to home through the tap. A stress-free nation with wonderful and 'happy go lucky people' living a fairy tale life.

Anything that has to do with beauty, perfection, elegance, grace, flawlessness, superiority, brilliance, wisdom, intelligence, and excellence, belongs to this mighty nation of the United States of America. We created all our mighty stories or you can call it theories using those positive adjectives and our wildest imaginations.

In those early ages of childhood, no one amongst ourselves had any idea about the American led war in Vietnam or even what happened in our closest neighboring nation of Somalia. The only thing I knew or we believed firmly to be real as kids was the fact that there is no single country in the entire world that can stand up to the United States of America. I always believed the US could occupy any nation with ease and bear no casualty at all. And these views are shaped by the stories we created and told.

In a part of the world where we need to worry about food, cloth, shelter, and many other necessities every day; in a world where a kid have to worry almost similarly with his parents about the ordeals of life; in a world where kids have some times need to work a daunting task in the house to support their families; our ideal fantasy child life was imagined by a all of us, as an American child life.

In our non-ending wild imaginations about this mighty nation, we used to talk about an ecstatic school kid in America with the perfect happy family, with many pairs of shoes, a lot of wardrobes or clothes to choose from, and a lot of meat/dairy products to eat from. We used to think kids in the US used to eat meat day and night.

When I think about it now It was a good thing that we did not know about stand alone rooms for kids in a big house in America, that story would have been a blast for our group in that time. Because no one would have believed everyone can get a room and bed to himself/herself. As a child our bedroom and living room used to be the same and the beds were just a piece of rug/mat.

These unbelievable imaginations that we had about The United States of America was our fantasy lifestyle as a kid in a third-world, least developed and impoverished country at the time. For instance, meat was always a luxury that our family could afford only during holidays. There are at least four national holidays that call for slaughtering a goat or a chicken or a shared oxen that could land us a feast of meat dishes when we were kids. Otherwise, getting meat on a dish is a very distant dream for most of us. That is may be why we used to think the kids in the US eat meat everyday.

In a very similar fashion to the mysterious meat dish clothes or shoes were also a once-in-a-year miracle. Most of the time we even have to choose between the two, it is either one pair of shoes or a cloth. My entire childhood I remember I only got a cloth to wear once a year which is just one pair and sometimes a shoe that may come once in two to three years on some occasions since we used to prioritize the clothes every year in order to look great. Since the shoes did not play much of a role in looking classy and fashionable, we only get them may be once in two or three years.

For me or for all of the kids in the small remote village of East Africa, America was the perfectly direct opposite of this pathetic, pitiful, sad and miserable looking life of us. We strongly believed school children in the United States of America get their choice of clothes, shoes and other wearables anytime in whatever amount they are interested in.

Back here in the third world food was also another luxury that is an issue for almost all household alike. Let alone consuming meat and other fancy food dishes, the ordinary daily meal itself was the mightiest challenge in every family throughout the country as it is in my own family.

So, we imagine kids in America eating fancy, and delicious meat dishes day and night without worrying a bit. (Thank God and those Ethiopian patriots who defeated Italians at the mighty battle of Adwa during Italy's attempt to colonize our nation in the 19th Century to make Ethiopia the only uncolonized African nation; we do not know about Pizzas, Burgers, Cakes and Chocolates at that time). The only thing we know about is those hard gained delicious meals and cuisines of Ethiopia authentic to the nation.

Moving away from home to the schools, our view of the United States of America was a government that provided schools with lavish buildings, Ph.D. holder teachers for all graders, encompassing lavish rooms, free delicious meals, high tech enabled classrooms, and easily and remotely accessible schools. Students with all the necessary equipment's and gadgets to ease their study.

As I repeatedly tried to indicate before, this was a reflection of mine and other kids' fantasy from the village. By the way, back here in Ethiopia we do get education for free from the government but we have to walk long distances on foot to get to the schools built by the government. And don't get carried away by the generosity of our government the classrooms we go to were built from what looked like total dirt. They are houses made from wood and mud and most of those classes do not have doors or windows.

As far as I remember those classrooms didn't have chairs or tables to sit and study on. We used to sit on large stones that we brought in from the wild. The classes were full of dust, the teachers were mean; scolding us at every chance they got. May be that is why we classified our elementary school teachers based on the level of their meanness. A school with no appropriate toilet for all let alone a lady and gents' classification. So, the whole idea of schools in America has to be imagined in a perfectly opposite way of these horror shows at our schools.

For instance, we always thought teachers of the mythical land of America to be very much nice and warm to kids. Beautiful classrooms with plenty of seats. Auspicious compound where kids are nurtured and enjoyed life to the fullest.

I still do remember fighting with my friends in an argument while debating about schools. The argument was the fact that in the US a classroom only has 20 to 30 students in one session. Other students who found my argument absurdly difficult to believe used to argue that it is impossible because we all know we study in a 5-meter square classroom and we were about 100 students in that classroom.

The issue of school amenities was totally another story to be told dearly here. We as a kid studied in schools with no books, no libraries, no laboratories, no play grounds (May be except a very vast grass land to run around). The only thing that made our school a school was may be the existence of students and teachers under one roof with a piece of wood painted black to serve as a board.

In order to study at those schools mentioned above having our personal study materials happen to be the sturdiest of all demanding determination and skills beyond a kid has to acquire. Getting our parents to buy us pens and pencils was the toughest negotiation that we have to go through in our childhood. Most of the time we have to perform some form of domestic work to get school amenities for school. We have to earn it by working for it since our bargaining power basically lies within our free labor only at that time of our age.

That is may be why in my mind I always thought the families in the United States are perfect for their children. I always thought they provided everything for their kids. Loving, affectionate, classy, adorable, accepting, stylish and more positive adjectives that we know of at that stage used to be associated with American families in our mind.

We also used to argue that if parents lay hands on their children or hit them the kids in the US can call the police and get their parents arrested. I don't really think this to be the case to this date though. I don't think children can just call police on their parents. This was because as a kid all Ethiopians maybe have been subjected to some form of domestic violence. Scolding or hitting by parents was considered morally right and a noble way to bring up a kid. In every typical Ethiopian household, it was normal to find a piece of rope made from an animal skin with a stick hanger. This piece of household furniture is basically used to discipline a child by beating. This rope is not some thing parents are ashamed of or try to hide at all, they clearly hang on the walls of the living house at every household in Ethiopia with pride. I still do not remember how many of those ropes of leather my parents used over the years to discipline me and my four siblings.

There was even a very famous expression if grownups or senior members of the society especially witness a child behaving differently or immorally; they used to say 'what lousy parents he/she had, if he/she had someone scolding them earlier they would not have been like this'.

The expression is signifying the glorification of domestic child abuse as an only way of disciplining children.

Punishing a child was a noble way to raise a child here in Ethiopia particularly and in Africa generally. So, the winning argument among my friends was that in America there is no such thing as punishing a kid violently. Because, if punished the government or the police will arrest the parent and look after the kid. As far as Ethiopia is concerned there are no social services here that look after the wellbeing of children at all. The only best option of social security here is to have a parent.

It was Later on in my life I came to my own conclusion that the social security system, the family structure and social dynamics in the United States we used to glorify and yearn for was not as fancy as we imagined though.

It is to be noted that by this time I have no idea what the government is or what it does or the types of governments or their nature, but with such myths about the United States of America, every one of us yearns to be there as a kid. We really wanted to leave our schools, and parents and live there just to escape the harsh reality of violence we face from our own loving but violent; affectionate but aggressive; and caring but fierce parents comparatively.

In my earliest years, all of this served as the foundation for my perception of America as the mightiest nation on earth. It is this foundation that would be tested as I journeyed through various life experiences, which played a significant role in shaping my views of America in the years to come and to this date.

All things being said though, I am not saying everything around me growing up was doom and gloom in that remote rural town of Eastern Ethiopia that has no connection to the outside world. I am just saying in comparison to what we had it was America first and may be America second and third too. Otherwise, I had an amazingly adventurous childhood filled with thrills, excitements, joys, cultural festivals, religious holidays unlike anywhere else, and many other exciting experiences of our own.

I think there is beauty in being a poor kid in a small remote rural town, because I cherish that we lived like we were hunters and gatherers. We used to explore the surrounding diverse natural forests looking for wild food. We skipped school and roamed around the forests, rivers, and beautiful green lushes to harvest wild fruits to eat and enjoy. We used to swim in ponds and take showers in an open river with no shyness to no one's end. We harvested plants we had no idea what they were and tasted all of them. We picked those that tasted good and approved them as a dessert on the weekends and after school. It is like we were discoverers on an expedition that came across great foods and things to do. These are may be our legacies that we hand down to the generation coming next to us as a kid. New exotic foods and new kind of plays. We also looted farmers for fresh fruits on the farm. Fruits like peaches, Guava, sugar apple, sugar cane, and countless other fruits were looted in a coordinated attack by group of friends fresh out of the farms. We also looted grains like fresh corn for roast sorghum cane after skipping classes. (Shout out to our dear farmers though, even if we were stealing their produce, they were only concerned about us destroying the foundation of the plant not the fruits we took).

Ethiopia as a nation and society might have came a very long way since those times registering one of the most remarkable economic growth and change in life standard but for us from the 90s all of the above remains true at every corner of the nation without any discrepancy.

Chapter two: America; late 1990s and New millennium

"America is the world's hope for the 21st century."
- George W. Bush, 2000

The dawn of the new millennium or the year 2000 G.C. for the entire world was one of the most important time or periods in the world history; except my country Ethiopia which entered the new century after eight years due to its unique calendar. By this time I had started to learn some English language, and I had started to watch some American movies and lots of Indian movies. Even though I was not very smart or knowledgeable, by this time I had started to distinguish what was realistic and what was not. Therefore, I and my friends' arguments about America had changed a lot during this period. We no longer believed in some of the myths that we used to tell each other as kids. We started to question and doubt some of the stories that we used to hear from others. We started to learn and discover some of the facts that we used to ignore or overlook.

Enter the era of Jean Claude Van-damme, Steven Seagal, Bruce Willis, Jackie Chan, Arnold Schwarzenegger, and many other action stars who introduced me and my gang to the world of movies from Hollywood through VHS tapes. These were the tapes that we watched on small TVs in a crowded room with no seat we call cinema.

NB: Possessing a television set and VHS player was akin to owning a treasure, a luxury that only a select few could afford in my town at that specific period of my life.

That was the age of action heroes. For someone who did not understand English, the only way we used to connect with the movies was through action. We did not care much about the plot or the dialogue or the characters. We only cared about the fights and the chases and the explosions and the stunts. We loved to see the action heroes beat up the bad guys and save the day and get the girl. We loved to see them use their skills and weapons and gadgets and vehicles. We loved to see them travel to different places and face different challenges and overcome different obstacles.

Our introduction to the world of cinema was through the local traditional movie theatres (I mean a room with a 21-inch television set) with no seats at all. These were the places where we went to watch movies with other kids like us. These were the places where we paid about 25 Ethiopian cents for a movie ticket (Well there is no ticket actually, it is just the owner of the TV at the gate collecting the cents and letting us in to that small room full of Kids). These were the places where we sat on the floor or stood on the walls or crowded on the windows. But for us these were the places where we had fun and excitement and thrill and joy.

In a way these American action movies showing American soldiers or any ordinary American fighting off Russians and other bad guys and winning somewhat magnified my original mythical thought of America again in a different way than the earlier version. I started to think that America is a country of heroes and warriors and champions. I thought that America was a country that fought for justice and freedom and peace. I thought that America was a country that always won against its enemies and always protected its allies. I thought that America was a country that had courage and strength and honor and glory.

Even the Indian movies I watched almost daily at those cinemas sometimes magnified America in my mind. These were the movies that showed Indian characters who lived in America or visited America or had some connection with America. These were the movies that showed America as a land of opportunity and prosperity and glamour and romance. These were the movies that showed America as a land of skyscrapers and bridges and monuments and parks that Bollywood actors go to for romancing their co actors in a glamorous way.

As I watched more and more movies from Hollywood, I started to form a totally new vivid and detailed picture of America in my mind. I started to see how America looked like and how Americans lived and how Americans acted through the eyes of American Action movies. I started to see the state-of-the-art schools, hospitals, roads, and so many other amenities that I had imagined before. I started to see the beautiful, lush, prosperous American communities and cities that I had dreamed about before.

The movies projected almost entirely a positive and ideal image of America and Americans. They showed me America as a land of freedom and democracy and opportunity and diversity. They showed me Americans as complete heroes, defenders of truth, equality and humanity. They showed me Americans as brave and smart and strong and good.

Those action movies portrayed mostly Russian bad guys trying to undermine the beauty of American lives and ordinary Americans standing against all the odds and defending. That was a mythical thing to do. It was like watching David versus Goliath, or Hercules versus Hydra, or Luke Skywalker versus Darth Vader. It was like watching a fairy tale or a legend or a myth come to life.

On the other hand, those action movies with actors playing spies for the American CIA also magnified my previous thought that Americans could dissipate any threat anywhere without being detected. Previously, in the early ages I used to think that was just because of the latest technology they had. But movies brought in another dimension where it was also because of the sheer bravery of an everyday ordinary American that this nation was such a mythical land.

Honoring the childhood traditions of gossip and children forum, After watching these over the top unrealistic action movies which we used to thought to be real; the first thing we used to do when we returned back to our village from the cinemas was retelling the whole story of the movie to other kids in the village who were mostly below our ages and those who could not afford the 25 cents. We used to narrate every scene and every dialogue and every action and every twist that we could remember. We used to imitate every gesture and every expression and every sound and every effect that we could reproduce. We used to exaggerate every detail and every emotion and every outcome and every impact that we could enhance.

We used to do this for two reasons: one, because we wanted to share our excitement and joy and wonder and awe with them. And two, because we wanted to impress them and amaze them and influence them and like we used to do before and our older brothers used to do before us. Having something that influences a bunch of kids in a magnificent way is all a kid could ask for in the age no grownup listens to what he/she says.

So as a kid, we wanted those kids to see what we saw and feel what we felt and think what we thought and dream what we dreamed. We wanted them to see America as we saw it, a mythical nation that had everything that we admired.

Most of the kids our age watched those movies occasionally when they got the 25 cents to pay for the movie theatre. So, the day one of us got lucky and got 25 cents, it would be that person's turn to brag and tell the story of the movie. It would be that person's chance to show off and entertain and amuse and influence the other kids.

In the process of retelling the movie to our peers in the village, there was always a competition to stand out from the rest of the friends just like we used to do in our story telling's I mentioned in the previous chapter. So, if I had a chance to retell a movie by Jean Claude Van Damme one day, I would even go to the extent of creating a totally fake action sequence to make the movie that I watched better than the one my friend watched the day before. I would add some extra kicks and punches and flips and jumps that were not in the original movie. I would make up some new characters and locations and weapons and gadgets that were not in the original movie. I would change some of the plot and dialogue and humour and drama that were not in the original movie just to stand out from the crowd.

The story retelling was an interesting phenomenon by itself, whereby we would try to recreate all the stunts and fight scenes by the words we had and some stunts of our own. We would use our body language and facial expressions and voice tones and sound effects to make our stories more vivid and exciting. We would use our imagination and creativity and memory and logic to make our stories more coherent and consistent.

Imagine a 9 to 10-year-old kid trying to explain Kick Boxer to a bunch of kids running around trying to show how Jean Claude Van-Damme trains. Making the sound of the kick on a face or somewhere else making the sound of something crash like boom or ka boom. Imagine how they would describe how Van Damme fights against his enemy who killed his brother. How we would describe how Van Damme uses his skills and strength and speed and courage to defeat him. How we would describe how Van Damme wins and avenges and celebrates and loves.

So most of the kids below our age who still didn't have access to movies like us would imagine the mightiest America in our stories. They would believe everything that we told them, without questioning or doubting or verifying or challenging (Well there is no way they can do that for that matter). They would accept everything that we showed them, without comparing or contrasting or analyzing or evaluating (Thank God we were all Kids). They would learn everything that we taught them, without exploring or discovering or experimenting or experiencing.

All their knowledge about America at this early stage would be manipulated by our narration mixed with fake stories of the movies in a plight to be the one with the greatest movie experience among the crowd. They would think that America was exactly like what we said it was, based on what we saw on the screen.

These retelling of stories of movies also had one other major problem. We as kids still did not differentiate between reality and fiction especially what goes behind in making the movies. We did not understand that movies were not real life, but only representations of life. We did not understand that movies were not facts, but only interpretations of facts. We did not understand that movies were not truth, but only versions of truth.

So, apart from the manipulation of the stories to stand out from the crowd even for us most of the heroics we saw on movies we thought were how all ordinary Americans lived. We thought that they were always fighting and saving and winning and loving. We thought that they were always heroes and warriors and champions and lovers.

By the way, as someone who grew up in the countryside, none of our friends or families owned a TV at this early age of ours. So, our first encounter with movies was at the local traditional 21-inch TV set cinema where only action movies from Hollywood and Bollywood played. The cinemas used to pack 100 kids in a room of 5 square meter sitting over each other to showcase the movies. This was the only place where we could watch movies, and this was the only type of movies that we could watch. We did not have any other options or alternatives or choices or preferences.

I had not seen any cartoon movies or animation, or kids shows at this time. So, it was impossible for me to imagine that those things I saw on TV were not realistic. I thought that everything that I saw on TV was real and true and factual and actual. I thought that everything that I saw on TV was happening somewhere in the world, especially in America. I thought that everything that I saw on TV was how people lived and acted and behaved and spoke.

I still even remember by the time TVs started to get into our houses in my teenage years elders like my mom used to say "Don't these people have jobs other than staying and talking in these TV, whole day" when they saw mostly white people in TVs. Even, they used to think that what they saw in TV were the real lives of people and they were amazed by it. They used to think that they were watching some kind of reality unfold on the screens. They used to think that they were watching some kind of window or portal or mirror or telescope into another world.

Above all, during this time movie choices were limited to action genre only because no one understood English. As far as language was concerned, Bollywood from India was an exception. Bollywood movies, whether they were romantic or action or drama, we used to watch them. Because we had some informal translators in the traditional small cinema of ours. I really don't know whether those guys spoke or knew Hindi (The Bollywood language) or not.

But from what I learned later, it was all about movies. Those translators learned Hindi because they watched lots of movies and turned to translators there and even earned some money for that service of translation. They watched the same movies over and over again, until they memorized the words and the meanings and the expressions and the emotions. They watched different movies with different genres and themes and styles and tones, until they learned the vocabulary and the grammar and the idioms and the slang.

I myself learned to speak and hear a little Hindi later, thanks to them. I learned some words and phrases and sentences and questions in Hindi. I learned some greetings and compliments and jokes and insults in Hindi. I learned some numbers and colours and animals and foods in Hindi.

I learned all this from watching Bollywood movies with informal translators in the traditional small cinema of ours. I learned all this without going to school or taking a class or reading a book or using an app. I learned all this without knowing how to read or write or spell or pronounce Hindi. I learned all this without having any native speakers or teachers or friends or relatives who spoke Hindi.

In those tiny, dusty cinemas with no more than a handful of seats and a modest 21-inch television set, the real power players were the translators. During our movie marathons, they held the remote control, and when the chatter got going, they'd hit pause and give us the lowdown on what was happening, usually in a pretty brief and to-the-point manner. Sometimes, it felt like they were using their creative flair to fill in the gaps! These were the folks who decided what to translate, what to skip, what to embellish, and what to tweak in the movies. They were the maestros of translation, choosing how to convey, explain, summarize, and even throw in their own commentary on the films. Now, they weren't too fussed about being spot-on or super precise; their top priorities were speed, simplicity, and keeping the entertainment factor high in their translations!

During long conversations in the movies they paused the movie and explained to us what was happening in a generally summarized way. I think sometimes they just translated based on their imagination of what was going on in a certain scene. They did not care much about the accuracy or the fidelity or the quality or the consistency of their translation as there is no one checking their legitimacy for that matter. They only cared about the speed and the simplicity and the clarity and the entertainment of their translation.

However, for Hollywood movies there was no such thing as translators. No one would agree to see if the cinema put up romantic or drama movies from Hollywood. No one was interested in those kinds of movies that had a lot of talking and a little action. No one was interested in those kinds of movies that had a lot of emotions and a little violence. No one was interested in those kinds of movies that had a lot of English that none of us understand and comprehend with easily.

Everyone was interested in action movies of Hollywood showing the mighty America in a bright light. It did not matter whether you knew the language or not, grown ups beating the hell out of each other was self explanatory and universal entertainer by itself. Everyone loved to see those kinds of movies that had a lot of action and a little talking. Everyone loved to see those kinds of movies that had a lot of violence and a little emotion. Everyone loved to see those kinds of movies that had a lot of simplicity and a little complexity.

And those choices of movies were actually made by older kids not the audience. They were the ones who had access to the video tapes or the VCRs or the cinemas. They were the ones who had money or connections or influence or power to get or rent or borrow or watch the movies. They were the ones who decided what movies to watch and when to watch and where to watch and with whom to watch.

One thing that requires a brief clarification here is that during this period, there were no PG-13 kind of restrictions. We watched every movie, literally every action flick that made its way to our town at that time. If you had 25 cents, you were in for the show – no questions asked. The only rule our town's movie theatres adhered to were the PG-25 rule (Only those with 25 cents could watch the movie). I vividly remember that even during the night-time, those cinemas would screen explicit adult films for anyone with at least 25 cents to spare. With no restrictions on what movies to watch, we formed our perception of ruthless, heroic, and triumphant Americans from those moving pictures.

In my life in general though the role American movies played is more of a positive one especially after I started to grasp some English and shifted towards watching drama movies and other non-action genres. I will be dedicating one chapter to the role of movies in my life later on. I will be explaining how movies helped me learn more about America and its culture and its history and its society. I will be explaining how movies helped me learn more about myself and my identity and my values and my goals. I will be explaining how movies helped me learn more about life and its challenges and its opportunities and its meanings.

This was how I watched America as a child, a mythical nation that had everything that I admired. In general, the earlier mythology we crafted about America through our childhood imaginations has been brought to life, becoming more realistic and vivid thanks to the magic of movies. America, as the unrivalled greatest nation in the world, was etched even more deeply into our minds, now adorned with information that looked strikingly realistic.

Chapter three: 9/11 and Iraq war

"Today, our nation saw evil – the very worst of human nature – and we responded with the best of America. With the daring of our rescue workers, with the caring for strangers and neighbors who came to give blood and help in any way they could."
–Then-President George W. Bush

FOR MOST OF THE WORLD, 9/11, that fateful September day, marked a pivotal moment that profoundly reshaped the lives of Americans and Westerners. However, at that time, few were conscious of, let alone studied, the far-reaching impacts of such events on diverse groups of people beyond the borders of the United States and the Western world. And if anyone did contemplate this expanded notion of going beyond the west, their focus was likely limited to how it directly affected individuals hailing from the Middle East or Muslim Arab nations.

Remarkably, the repercussions of the September 11th attack extend even further, encompassing a more extensive list of societies affected by the incident. Surprisingly, my own society finds its place on that list, as the attack left an indelible mark on my childhood in one of the smallest towns in Eastern Ethiopia. At that time, our town was home to no more than 20,000 residents. It may come as a surprise to consider how the life of a child in an Eastern African nation, nestled in a quiet corner of a small town, could be influenced by the seismic events of 9/11, but it most certainly was. Allow me to explain:

In Ethiopia, the religious landscape is predominantly defined by two major faiths: Christianity and Islam. It's a nation that proudly wears its religious identity, and you'd be hard-pressed to find a more devout country anywhere in the world. Over 99% of the Ethiopian population identifies as religious believers. However, my perspective on religion was quite distinct during my formative years, around the age of 10 or 11, which would be in the year 2000 G.C. or before the harrowing events of the Taliban attack on September 11th.

Ethiopia is a country where Christians and Muslims coexist harmoniously, living side by side in peace and unity. I was born into a Christian family, and some of my own relatives held positions as priests in the Ethiopian Orthodox Church. Yet, I was raised with a deep respect for Islam and its sacred traditions. One notable practice that reflected this respect was our response to the Muslim call to prayer, known as the 'Azan', emanating from the nearby mosque.

Whenever the hauntingly beautiful sound of the 'Azan' echoed through the air, whether it be dawn, midday, or evening, a peculiar ritual unfolded in our household. We would promptly silence any radio or Television within our home and patiently wait until the call to prayer had concluded. This wasn't a formal law or rule bestowed upon us by some one, but rather a cherished habit that my family and neighbors held dear. We undertook this gesture as an expression of our profound reverence for Allah/God and those engaged in His worship.

Interestingly, there were no Muslim families residing immediately adjacent to us, yet we upheld this tradition as a heartfelt demonstration of respect for our fellow citizens who followed the Islamic faith.

In addition to my family's respect for Islam, I was fortunate to have many Muslim friends during my upbringing. We shared moments of play and learning together, forging bonds that transcended religious boundaries. To us, the distinctions between our faiths were almost inconsequential. It was our firm belief that we were all, in essence, worshiping the same divine Creator, only using different languages and approaches to express our devotion. In the tapestry of our lives, our diverse faiths blended seamlessly into a harmonious and colorful whole.

For example, we held a charming misconception. We believed that the commonly used Christian phrase 'In the name of the Father; the Son, and The Holy Spirit' (spoken in Amharic or our local language version by the Christians) was akin to the prayerful common phrase Muslims uttered during their devotions: 'Bismillah Ir-Rahman Ir-Rahim' (in Arabic: بِسْمِ ٱللَّهِ ٱلرَّحْمَٰنِ ٱلرَّحِيمِ).

'Bismillah Ir-Rahman Ir-Rahim' translates to 'In the name of God, the Merciful, the Compassionate.' (Which I found out very late in my age). This beautiful Arabic phrase serves as both an invocation and an expression of faith for Muslims. It's recited before they embark on any endeavor or commence their reading of the Quran, a heartfelt acknowledgment of their gratitude and devotion to God.

Back then, as children, the depth of these phrases and their subtle nuances eluded our comprehension. We simply operated under the assumption that both expressions were calls to invoke God's name and seek His blessings before embarking on any endeavor under different language and religion. The intricacies and distinctions between them remained veiled from our youthful understanding. It wasn't until later that we came to realize that while the words themselves differed, there is also a greater distinction that felt irreconcilable.

One of the most cherished memories of my childhood revolves around a delightful moment when my Muslim friends and I attempted to align the two translations of the phrases we employed to invoke God's name and seek His blessings before embarking on any endeavor. It was a moment filled with youthful curiosity and boundless joy, as we eagerly compared our respective faiths. I remember to tell my Muslim friends that a Priest from our Church and a Sheik from their Mosque translating the common Christian phrase and the common Muslim phrase to be similar and rejoicing on that fact.

In our shared exploration, we found a sense of delight and astonishment. Discovering that our two religions, though expressed in different languages, resonated with such harmonious similarity filled us with an inexplicable joy. While we may not have fully comprehended the exact meanings or nuances behind these phrases at the time, the connection and resemblance between them transcended mere words. It was a beautiful testament to the common threads that bound us as friends and believers, irrespective of the languages we spoke or the paths we followed in our faith.

This harmony and unity held particularly true in the Eastern Ethiopian region where my upbringing took place, a place characterized by religious diversity and peaceful coexistence. In this vibrant tapestry, Christians and Muslims lived side by side, not just peacefully but with profound respect for one another's beliefs and practices. We didn't merely tolerate our differences; we celebrated them, weaving a rich fabric of diversity into the fabric of our daily lives.

In this cultural mosaic, we wholeheartedly embraced each other's festivals and traditions, inviting one another to partake in the joyous celebrations. We shared not only our meals but the stories of our faith, deepening our understanding of one another's beliefs.

A particularly heartwarming example of this unity was evident during the Muslim observance of Ramadan. Christian friends would willingly join their Muslim friends in the fasting, not out of compulsion, but as a voluntary testament of their love and respect. It was a remarkable expression of solidarity that transcended religious boundaries. After breaking the fast together, we would spend the entire night reveling in each other's company, partaking in games and joyous moments. It felt like a vibrant celebration of life, faith, and the unbreakable bonds of friendship that connected us.

As an example, another lasting instinct from my childhood remains with me to this day – the instinct to avoid walking in front of a Muslim in prayer. This fundamental gesture of respect was ingrained in me by my family and neighbors, who imparted upon me the values of reverence towards Islam and its sacred practices.

Likewise, I fondly recall the beautiful traditions of shared love and goodwill between our families and those of our Muslim friends. During Ethiopian Easter or at the conclusion of the two-month fasting period observed by Orthodox Christians, our Muslim friends' families would extend warm gestures of friendship by gifting us with offerings such as chicken, eggs, and other food items. These acts of generosity transcended religious boundaries and exemplified the bonds of love and camaraderie that united us.

At the age of ten, in the heart of my formative years, the distinction between Christians and Muslims was a trivial matter. In my eyes, we were all kindred spirits, bound by a shared love for God, albeit expressed through two different languages and faiths. It was a testament to the unity and love that transcended our religious affiliations.

Enter; September 11!

Regrettably, the impact of the September 11th incident reached our small town in Ethiopia in ways we could never have imagined. It was an incredible upheaval stemming from thousands of kilometers away in the United States, shaking the very foundations of our lives. 9/11 bore witness to a transformation that forever altered the harmonious diversity we had cherished for so long. It brought with it a wave of fear, suspicion, hatred, and violence, a stark contrast to the friendship and camaraderie that once bound us as friends and neighbors.

In the aftermath of this tragic event, our beliefs and identities were cast into the crucible of doubt. For the first time, I found myself confronted with the unsettling reality of Muslims and Christians harboring animosity towards one another, strangers in a land where they had once been comrades. It was my first encounter with the concept of terrorism, particularly ascribed to Muslim terrorists, and it left a deep impression on my young mind. The narrative of Muslims seeking to convert or destroy Christians, casting Islam as a violent and oppressive faith at odds with the principles of Christianity, entered my consciousness.

This revelation about the perceived antagonism between these two faiths shook me to my core. It challenged the very essence of my worldview. Suddenly, the familiar sound of the five daily prayer calls from the mosque, which I had always respected, took on a different tone. The character I had developed, one that refrained from crossing in front of a praying Muslim out of respect, was now put to the test. Everything I once held dear and understood was subjected to a profound and bewildering transformation.

I want to emphasize that the views I'm sharing now aren't necessarily representative of everyone, especially the older generation, and I can't be certain about their perspectives. However, what I'm trying to convey is the profound impact that 9/11 had on a 10-year-old child growing up in a remote East African town.

Almost overnight, America ceased to be a distant land; we started to see them as part of 'us.' This transformation stemmed from the fact that, like us, they were Christians. We felt that one of our own had been targeted by those who identified as Muslims. In the eyes of Christian children in our village, our perception of Muslim kids began to shift. We began to see them as somehow aligned with the notion of Arabs 'destroying' Christians, and we considered ourselves as righteous Christians, standing in alliance with fellow believers, including those in countries like the USA, in a sort of partnership for the Kingdom of God.

During this period, we witnessed a notable change in our community. Many Muslim parents in our area chose to name their newborns 'Sadam' or 'Osama,' a reflection of the tumultuous times and perhaps an expression of their own complex feelings. Moreover, our once-unified daily playtime began to show cracks, revealing the creeping divide along religious lines within our group of friends.

Muslim children started perceiving us, the Christians, as supporters of America, while we, in turn, sometimes cast the Muslim children as if they were all somehow aligned with the Taliban and other figures from the Arab world. It was as if a shadow of suspicion had descended upon us, dividing our once-joyful play into an unsettling contest of 'us versus them.'

As if to further deepen the rift, the consecutive wars in Afghanistan and Iraq played out on the global stage, amplifying the divides within our Christian and Muslim communities. These events fueled more suspicion, giving rise to fear, hatred, and animosity that hung heavy in the air, casting a cloud over the bonds we had once cherished.

I still have vivid recollections of small-scale demonstrations that took place in my humble hometown, home to around 20,000 residents, protesting the American invasions of Iraq and Afghanistan. These demonstrations were notable for their timing; they usually occurred on Fridays, following the weekly Jumma Muslim prayer, and often began at the local mosques.

The curious aspect was that, at the time, our town had no foreign residents, and there was no presence of any media outlet within our locality. This led us to wonder about the intended audience of these demonstrations. Naturally, it was widely assumed, if not unanimously believed, that the messages conveyed were aimed primarily at the Christian community within our town.

For the Christians in our town during those times, a cloud of apprehension, confusion, and a sense of being inadvertently victimized hung heavily in the air. The unfolding events had left us feeling anxious about our place in a world suddenly filled with tensions and division.

On the flip side, within the Christian community, there was a palpable sense of pride in identifying themselves with the mightiest nation on Earth, the United States. Many took pride in seeing the USA as a Christian country, a guardian of Christian values and the Christian world. However, it's important to note that this notion, while held dear by some, can sometimes be far from the reality, as Ethiopians perceive America's brand of Christianity in a different light, a perspective I'll delve into in subsequent chapters.

What makes it somewhat comical, looking back, is that most of the people in our small town didn't truly grasp the full scope of what was happening globally. For us, living in a remote corner of East Africa, it was distilled down to a seemingly simplistic war between Muslims and Christians. Yet, the reality was far more complex and nuanced, with geopolitical motives at play. It wasn't a religious war, but that understanding would come to me much later in life, along with the revelation that the CIA had trained figures like Bin Laden, adding another layer of complexity to the narrative.

Even within the Christian population of Ethiopia, the majority are devout followers of the Ethiopian Orthodox Church, one of the world's oldest Christian denominations. During the specific time when I was a child, around the 9/11 attacks and the subsequent wars, there was a certain animosity, often bordering on disdain, directed towards a specific religious group. Ironically, this group wasn't even Muslims; it was the Protestant Christians.

What makes this irony more intriguing is that, at the time, I don't believe most of the Ethiopian Christians were fully aware that the United States, a nation they looked up to, was predominantly a Protestant dominated country.

It leaves me pondering where the support of the Christian community would have aligned if they had possessed a clearer understanding of the religious dynamics at play in the United States.

It was as though within the confines of our homes, there was an unspoken allegiance to always root for America to prevail in its endeavors. However, outside our homes, conversations surrounding these topics were almost non-existent. This was largely because the Christian community in Eastern Ethiopia constituted a very small minority, accounting for less than 2% of the population.

In hindsight, I can't help but find it amusing when I realize that the American wars in Afghanistan and Iraq had little to do with religion, despite the profound impact they had on our small, insulated world. It's almost comical to think that these grand geopolitical maneuvers were, in essence, a stage for the machinations of powerful politics, far removed from the simple perceptions that once shaped our thoughts.

What's even more amusing is that neither America nor the key players in those wars seemed to have any inkling about our existence in that remote town. No one seemed concerned about whether we supported their cause or not. The level of misconception and confusion within both the Orthodox Christians and the Protestant Christians, who harbored mutual animosities, and their perceptions of Islam and the United States, adds a layer of humor to the entire scenario that is difficult to put into words.

Amidst the bewildering swirl of misconceptions and confusion, one thing became painfully clear: suspicion had taken root among neighbors, fear had been sown, and a sense of unease pervaded our once-peaceful, diverse, tolerant, and beautifully harmonious community in a small town in East Africa.

It brings a cynical smile to my face when I reflect on the narratives I was fed about terrorism and the imminent global threats from Sadam Hussein and his weapons of mass destruction. In retrospect, I can't help but chuckle at the realization that many of these stories were, in a sense, part of an American script rather than any clear depiction of the other side. It's a stark reminder of how narratives and perceptions can be shaped and reshaped by powerful forces, often with unintended consequences.

All of these misconceptions that took root within us were the result of a multitude of influences. As children, we were like sponges, absorbing the narratives that surrounded us every day. These narratives flowed from our elders, echoed in school, resonated in the stories told in cinemas, reverberated through our village, found their way into our homes, and even filled the hallowed halls of our churches and mosques.

Our understanding of the world was shaped by these diverse sources of information, often without the critical discernment that comes with age and experience. It was a complex tapestry of ideas and beliefs woven together from the threads of our surroundings.

Amidst this tapestry of misconceptions, I feel a profound need to offer my sincere condolences and pay my respects. I want to remember not only the victims of the 9/11 attacks but also the countless innocent lives that were deeply affected by the subsequent wars in Iraq and Afghanistan. These were tragic chapters in our shared human history, marked by loss, suffering, and a collective longing for a more peaceful and just world.

So, at this time, my view about America is still that it is the greatest nation on earth. It has also become one of us. It was a surreal moment when we started to identify with this mighty nation, and even more amusing that the Muslims in our community are designating us American allies. It was great.

America became even more mighty and great in our minds climbing the ladder very high up, as a protector of Christianity. It is not just great at this time it is also one of us as a Christian protector.

Chapter four: Satellite TV and English

"The advent of satellite television has turned the planet into a global village. It's as if we now have a front-row seat to the world's stage."
- Rupert Murdoch

IN THE EARLY 2000S, a new and exciting world began to unfold before me as satellite television made its way into our lives through channels from Arabsat and Nile sat, transmitted from Middle Eastern countries. Among these channels, MBC stood out, offering a continuous stream of Hollywood movies, 24 hours a day, completely free of charge. This was my second gateway into the enchanting realm of Hollywood after the age of action heroes, and through it, I was introduced to a near-perfect depiction of America.

Among the movies that became regular fixtures on the screen were iconic titles like Titanic, Akeelah and the Bee, What Women Want, Bad Boys, Nutty Professor, Speed, The Matrix, Independence Day, and Ace Ventura. This was way before I delved into the realms of actors like Denzel Washington or Meryl Streep, nor had I fully explored the diverse genres of comedy, romance, or action that Hollywood had to offer. It was a captivating introduction to American cinema, one that would shape my perspective in the years to come away from the views I garnered via action heroes.

In addition to those movies from different genres Wrestling, in particular, became an integral part of virtually every household thanks to satellite television. By this point in the decade, television sets accompanied by satellite receivers had begun to find their way into many households, although mine had yet to receive this technological upgrade. So, I have to visit the better off neighbors house to get my dose of adrenaline from Hollywood.

On the screen, larger-than-life figures like Arnold Schwarzenegger, Sylvester Stallone, aka Rambo, the Blade franchises, Jackie Chan, Jet Li, and numerous other action stars and movies also took center stage and found their way to homes from those small screen PG-25 cinemas I told you before. It's interesting to note that if I were to mention the names of Hollywood actors here, it's quite possible that no one would recognize them because in our small town, we had a peculiar way of naming movie stars. We bestowed unique monikers upon these actors, names that were known only within the confines of our town and hardly recognized even just ten miles away.

FOR ME, THE MOVIES on satellite TV, particularly those outside the action genre, served as my first informal school for spoken English. Listening to Akeelah spell it out on the spelling bee championship helped me develop my vocabulary, watching Ace Ventura hilariously playing around with animal and people gave me an in-depth listening skill in English.

The thing is, in that small town where I grew up, the approach to teaching English in formal education, which we received for free in the public schools I mentioned in the first chapter, resembled that of mathematics more than a language of conversation or communication.

English classes were often delivered in a manner that felt more like solving mathematical equations. It was a style of teaching that unfortunately led many kids, including myself, to develop a certain aversion to studying English. This is a phenomenon very common across the country except may be in the urban areas where private sector education is common and better-quality education is delivered.

Just imagine each and every class session of English being a series of mathematical formulaic equations:

- verb + Ing =?
- Adjective + [variable] =?
- Pronouns + [variable] =?

This approach didn't cultivate a natural love for the language; instead, it made English feel like a puzzle to be solved. Unfortunately, for most of the kids, including myself, who have always found mathematics confusing and boring, English became one branch of mathematics adding another subject to hate in school.

What added to the challenge was the fact that many of our English teachers themselves did not have a strong command of the English language either, and often, they struggled to fully grasp the content of the course materials. As a result, they tended to place disproportionate emphasis on the most perplexing part of the syllabus, which was invariably the grammar section. I remember our English text books each chapter were classified into reading, writing, listening, speaking and Grammar. But only the grammar section was used to be taught by our teachers leaving the other sub sections totally aside. Unfortunately, this grammar section was primarily explained in a manner akin to solving mathematical equations in a complex manner.

This predicament as I said was not unique to my town; it was a widespread issue across Ethiopia. With the exception of children from the capital city of Addis Ababa, where many private schools offered a different educational experience, English proficiency among Ethiopian kids was often quite poor. The challenges in teaching and learning English ran deep, making it more of a theoretical exercise than a practical tool for communication.

Despite starting our English education from the early grades, it was a common experience that most of us still had a relatively low command of English by the time we reached college. The challenges in the educational system, particularly in the teaching of English, were significant.

However, for some fortunate individuals, including myself, a beacon of hope emerged in the form of satellite TV movies transmitted via Middle Eastern satellite television channels showcasing Hollywood films. These movies proved to be a lifeline for my English language skills. In particular, my listening and spoken skills saw remarkable improvement thanks to the hours spent engrossed in those films. They offered a real-world application of the language that was sorely lacking in the traditional classroom setting.

With the advent of this newfound 'school of English' through satellite TV movies, my approach to the language underwent a profound transformation. I began to view English through a lens entirely distinct from the mathematical approach prevalent in our formal education. These movies injected a sense of practicality and real-world relevance into my language learning journey.

This shift in perspective had a significant impact on my subsequent English classes. No longer did I perceive English as a mere set of mathematical equations to decipher, but rather as a living, dynamic means of communication. This change in mindset made my English classes considerably more accessible and enjoyable, as I had developed a deeper connection with the language.

I gradually phased out the habit of mechanically pairing verbs with various elements to achieve the correct grammatical structure before I spoke. Instead, I found myself making sense of sentences presented to me, drawing upon skills I had honed through hours of watching Hollywood movies. I could now identify the right grammatical combinations with a sense of intuition.

It's worth noting that, despite being an average student in most subjects throughout my primary and secondary education, there was one area where I consistently outperformed even the top students in the class—English. I owe this achievement entirely to the influence of Hollywood movies. They not only made me approach English with ease but also allowed me to master it with a profound sense of enjoyment. They transformed the way I engaged with the language, turning it from a classroom subject into a lifelong passion.

I have vivid memories of confounding my English teachers during speaking exercises, thanks to the impeccable pronunciations and vocabulary that I had absorbed from countless hours of watching movies. At times, I would even playfully deceive my teachers during presentations with an appearance of sophisticated English.

It's worth noting that, given that many of our teachers themselves struggled with English, they were often easily swayed by the facade of my presentations. These presentations weren't necessarily rich in content or a display of exceptional presentation skills; instead, they were bolstered by my newfound proficiency in English, which I had acquired through the medium of movies.

It's important to highlight a rather peculiar notion that prevails in countries like Ethiopia, where fluency in English is often equated with intelligence. In such cultural contexts, the ability to speak English eloquently is viewed as a hallmark of intellectual prowess.

As children, we often witnessed a curious dynamic in our households. Parents, in our community, would reprimand their children if they didn't speak English correctly or fluently, considering it a matter of great importance. Conversely, parents whose children displayed proficiency in well-spoken English would beam with pride and eagerly share their accomplishment with everyone around them.

The enduring belief that English proficiency equates to intelligence continues to be a prevailing aspect of everyday life, even to this day particularly in Ethiopia and may be generally in Africa.

Whether it's a politician addressing the public, an artist expressing themselves, or a businessman engaging with the media, there remains a common practice of incorporating English phrases into lengthy speeches in local languages. Such moments are often perceived as displays of intelligence, and those who listen tend to assume that individuals who seamlessly integrate English into their discourse are well-educated.

Individuals delivering speeches often employ these English remarks as markers of their superior intellect, utilizing them as a means to persuade and convince their audience.

Picture a football (Soccer for an American reader) commentator hosting a radio show in the local language, but peppering their commentary with terms like 'pass,' 'forward,' 'dribble,' 'transfer window,' 'accuracy,' and many others borrowed from English commentators. This commentary is delivered to an audience that may have little to no command of the English language, creating a unique blend of confusing languages that might not be understood by the local football enthusiasts.

In another example of English centricity I recall a memorable incident where the nation's Prime Minister once publicly scolded a Member of Parliament for pronouncing 'Fiscal policy' as 'Physical policy.' The Prime Minister, known for his own proficiency in English, took the opportunity to belittle the MP's mistake during a live television appearance, taking pride in his ability to elucidate the correct pronunciation of fiscal policy.

It's fascinating to contemplate the contrasting approaches to persuasive speech. In English, there are specific skills and techniques used to engage and persuade the audience effectively. However, in my country, when delivering speeches in local languages, it often suffices to sprinkle the discourse with catchy English words and phrases to create the illusion of persuasion. Remarkably, despite the simplicity of this approach, it does manage to sway some individuals, underscoring the unique dynamics of language and persuasion.

Another anecdote that never fails to amuse me is one my mom shared from the late 2000s. During that time, our town's administration decided to address the issue of unemployment among housewives, including my mom. They formulated a plan to offer credit facilities, backed by the government, to empower women to establish cooperative businesses.

In accordance with my mom's recollection, the incident unfolded when the mayor of our town extended an invitation to approximately ten unemployed housewives, including my mom, from our street. The women entered the mayor's office, where he occupied his customary seat at the managerial table. A desktop computer stood resolutely in front of him, its screen casting a faint glow across the room.

As the meeting commenced, with the mayor addressing the group of unemployed women in a local language of 'Afan Oromo' , an intriguing pattern emerged in his communication. Throughout the entirety of the meeting, the mayor seemed to favor certain phrases and expressions from English, using them as linguistic crutches. Words like 'Okay,' 'Very,' 'Very,' and 'Here' and many more peppered his explanations as he unveiled the ambitious initiative designed to empower the women.

ANOTHER INTRIGUING aspect of that meeting was the mayor's persistent tapping on the keyboard of the desktop computer. It was an era when internet connectivity was not readily available in our town. The mayor's continuous keyboard activity, coupled with his liberal use of English words during the meeting, seemed to be part of a conscious effort to assert his authority as an intellectual.

However, this attempt had an unintended consequence. My mother, who was illiterate but not easily fooled, couldn't help but suspect that the mayor might be putting on a show. She found his actions rather amusing and didn't hesitate to poke fun at him for the remainder of the year.

This practice of using English as a means to assert authority is prevalent across various levels of authority in our nation. I vividly recall instances where Members of Parliament openly chastised each other during parliamentary sessions for any misstep in the usage of English words within their speeches or discussions as I mentioned earlier.

ALLOW ME TO RECOUNT the true incident that unfolded within the highest governing body of a nation of 100 million people I started to narrate earlier in full now. In Ethiopia, the government operates under a parliamentary system where approximately 500 Members of

Parliament convene in the House of Peoples' Representatives to deliberate and make decisions.

I distinctly remember a televised episode where an opposition MP sought to highlight the irregularities within the Ethiopian Fiscal and Monetary policies during a session attended by none other than the Prime Minister. However, as this MP spoke, the words 'fiscal policy' repeatedly emerged from their lips but were pronounced in a manner that sounded more like 'physical' or 'Fiz'kal.'

When the time arrived for the Prime Minister to respond to the questions posed by the MPs, instead of addressing the pressing issues facing his government, he chose to make fun of the MP's pronunciation. His remarks sparked a riot of laughter within the parliament, which was predominantly controlled by the ruling party.

The entire chamber echoed with laughter as the esteemed opposition MP, who also happened to be a renowned professor of political science in the country, struggled with the pronunciation of 'fiscal policy.' Regrettably, amidst the laughter, the substantive question raised by the MP was overshadowed, and the nation found itself chuckling at the seemingly insignificant matter of language proficiency rather than engaging with the critical topics of fiscal and monetary policy.

Ethiopia, as a nation, holds English in such reverence that encountering someone speaking it fluently in public can evoke looks of awe, as if witnessing a miraculous event. English is undeniably a significant asset in my country, and for a young boy hailing from a small town like myself, mastering it often seems like an insurmountable challenge—one that typically requires nothing short of a miracle or the extraordinary influence of Hollywood. It is for this reason that I perpetually attribute the pivotal role Hollywood played in my life, effectively serving as my unconventional language school.

However, it's important to acknowledge that the perception I formed about America was also influenced in a somewhat skewed manner by those very movies that taught me English.

At that stage in my life, I witnessed what seemed like an idyllic portrayal of America. Concepts such as slavery in America, the struggles for Black rights, the civil liberty movements, or the deeply ingrained racial discrimination that characterizes American society were completely foreign to me. I had no inkling about the harsh reality of police brutality.

The America I knew from those movies, transmitted via Middle Eastern satellite television, appeared to be a land of perfection, peace, humor, and hope—an America I could wholeheartedly admire. Whether the movie choices made by the Middle Eastern channels were deliberate or not, they painted a picture of America that was utterly appealing.

For me, movies became more than just entertainment; they were a lifeline. The addiction I developed to Hollywood and Bollywood films served as my refuge during the toughest of times. These movies were my unwavering therapists, capable of helping me momentarily forget the grim realities of dire poverty and the relentless struggles I endured. As I watched the captivating depictions of lavish Western lifestyles on the silver screen, my own personal hardships would fade into the background, if only for a while.

However, America through those movies again soared very much higher and higher in my mind as the one and only greatest nation on earth. A country I once admired as mythical has now become a real myth characterized by free, happy, and just people that I came to know through those carefully selected looking movies.

The country I once admired as a land of heroes and Christian protector has now become the highest standard of morality and ethics in the world for me. Thanks to those movies selection Americans were engraved in my mind as a people with higher moral grounds and utmost ethics while people like Russians and middle eastern always look immoral and irresponsible.

While, Hollywood takes all the credit for being my free English school it is also responsible for my misconception about America for times to come. And also responsible for many other positive developments in my life as an individual and member of the society.

Chapter five: My first encounter with an American

"Meeting Americans for the first time is like meeting the whole world at once. Their diversity, optimism, and energy are a testament to the boundless possibilities of the human spirit."
- G.K. Chesterton

IN THE EARLY 2000S, around 2003 or 2004, I had the remarkable opportunity to meet Americans in person for the very first time in my life. It was an unforgettable encounter with two wonderful ladies hailing from San Diego, California. They arrived in our charming little town as volunteers, dedicating their time to teach English at our local school. This encounter marked the beginning of my journey into understanding America from a unique perspective.

Among those two remarkable ladies one of the lady was a teacher at a local elementary school in the US while the second and the energetic younger one was a student at a college in the United States.

These two people from San Diego California were one of the most amazing human beings I have ever encountered in my entire life.

Even though their time with us at the local school was short-lived, I remember the time I spent with both of them more vividly than the years I spent with my permanent teachers during most of my childhood. Both of these American ladies left a lasting impression that transcended the constraints of time.

They were not just smart and intelligent; they embodied a unique blend of energy, sweetness, and all the positive qualities one could hope to find in a fellow human being. Their passion for teaching and their genuine interest in our community's well-being were evident in every interaction we had with them.

The younger volunteer from the college was a truly exceptional teacher who revolutionized my perception of education. Her teaching style was nothing short of extraordinary. She brought boundless energy into the classroom, leaping around, cheering, and engaging with all of us while imparting English vocabulary. May be she is one of the reason among plenty for my ardent love of teaching which I practiced for almost a decade.

What set this young beautiful teacher apart was the sheer enthusiasm she radiated when we responded correctly to her questions. Her joy and exhilaration at our achievements were nothing short of infectious. I had never encountered a teacher who celebrated a student's success with such unrestrained delight. My elementary school teachers would give their life before complementing a student for an achievement.

The love and happiness she radiated during her time with us still resonate with me as if it were just yesterday. It was like a fairy god mother from the movies enchanting our haunted school run by mean scolding and unloving teachers.

I recall how she marveled at the impressive vocabulary command exhibited by some of us in the class. Credit undoubtedly goes to Hollywood, as the exposure to American movies by a few of us had enriched our English language skills. We eagerly claimed every piece of candy and chocolate she brought as a prize for our linguistic prowess. She, in turn, was the catalyst for expanding our vocabulary during her brief stay.

What truly set her apart was her ability to transform English class into an enjoyable, fun, and euphoric experience. Her teaching style was a breath of fresh air, especially for us at the school. These moments remain etched in my memory, and I continue to treasure them to this day.

In my entire elementary school experience, the teachers I encountered were known for their sternness, adhering to a strict "no laughter, no talking" policy. Schools, it seemed, were structured more like military camps, where a group of young children was being groomed to become disciplined adults. The teachers wielded a piece of chalk to write on the blackboard and, more ominously, a large stick to enforce discipline.

The atmosphere in these schools was formal and rigid, and humor or playfulness was a rarity. The contrast between this traditional approach to education and the exuberant teaching style of the American volunteer was stark, leaving a lasting impression on all of us.

In those days, we had no concept of teachers laughing and playing with their students. For us, every classroom session felt like a dangerous mission to survive without incurring the wrath of our teachers. Some teachers were so strict that they didn't even allow bathroom breaks, turning each class into a battle of endurance.

However, my American teacher defied all these norms. She was a complete contrast to our usual instructors. She exuded friendliness, humor, intelligence, and a deep appreciation for her students.

Her vibrant presence in our classroom was a breath of fresh air. I can still vividly recall her leaping from one desk to another, like an exuberant child. In our usual academic environment, such freedom of expression was unheard of.

We were conditioned to be reserved, not just at school but also in interactions with teachers and even within our families. However, the year 2003 marked a significant departure from the norm. It introduced us to a free-spirited American, a beacon of love and happiness who brought a sense of liberation to our small, often somber classrooms.

The second teacher we had was an older, experienced elementary school teacher from San Diego, and she was equally exceptional. She possessed a warm and caring personality that endeared her to everyone. As a Mexican American, she exuded both beauty and charm, drawing the attention of many young men from our town whenever she ventured outside the school premises.

These young men, although unable to communicate with her due to the language barrier, made attempts to engage with her. She might not have comprehended their words, but perhaps she sensed the admiration in their gestures. It was a testament to the idea that sometimes, human connections can transcend language.

Inside the classroom, she displayed a maternal care that resonated deeply with us children. Her nurturing demeanor made us feel cherished and safe. It was like my amazingly loving mother becoming an intellect and started teaching me English.

One of the most significant moments that remains etched in my memory from her class was the eye-opening reality check she provided about life in America. It is one such moment that shattered my deep rooted misconception about the mighty America from the most trustworthy mother like individual.

On occasion, she would candidly share her own personal challenges and struggles as a teacher in the United States. These narratives were nothing short of a revelation for my young and misinformed mind. Prior to her revelations, I had held a naive belief that the U.S. paid its teachers the highest salaries and that life there was marked by ease and prosperity for teachers.

I distinctly remember her detailing the hardships teachers faced in the U.S., including the difficulties they encountered in meeting their everyday needs. This was a profound shock to my system. I had firmly believed that American teachers were generously compensated for their work. Her candid discussions not only shattered that misconception but also made me rethink many of my assumptions about life in the United States of America.

I vividly recall a particular instance when she shared a personal story about her journey in the United States. She spoke about saving money to purchase her first car, using it as a powerful lesson on the importance of saving. This revelation opened my eyes to a reality I had never considered before. It is not a revelation about savings as you might have expected, it was about my misconception about the United States of America rather.

Until that moment, I had held the belief that in the United States, everyone could effortlessly acquire cars and homes. It was a misconception I had nurtured, likely influenced by the glamorous portrayals of American life in movies. The notion that people in the United States faced struggles and had to work hard to achieve their life goals was a revelation that fundamentally shifted my perspective. And that from the most trustworthy person from my viewpoint made it a sure thing.

It was in those moments, listening to this extraordinary teacher, that I began to see America in a more nuanced light, realizing that, like any other place in the world, it had its own set of challenges and triumphs. It was an awakening to the complexities of life beyond the silver screen.

It dawned on me that my previous notion of life in the U.S. had been overly simplistic. I had believed that prosperity was abundant and easily attainable in America, oblivious to the fact that people, even teachers, had to work diligently to make ends meet.

THE REALITY THAT EMERGED was a revelation, challenging my preconceived notions about the United States. I had grown up in a community where families who received financial support from relatives living in the U.S. were considered privileged. It seemed like a beacon of prosperity.

As I spent more time with these two remarkable English teachers, my desire to visit the United States intensified. San Diego, in particular, held a special place in my imagination. I longed for those joyful and educational moments in their classes, where I had learned not just English but also valuable life lessons.

I distinctly recall both of them graciously sharing their addresses with us. Although we never attempted to correspond through letters, I did make an effort to locate them online, particularly on Facebook, after some time had passed. However, my searches proved fruitless, leaving me to wonder if they might have outgrown the platform, given that it emerged just one year after our memorable encounter.

YET, ONE FUNDAMENTAL truth remains: the way I perceive education underwent a profound transformation at the hands of these remarkable American women creating a newfound animosity when going back to our normal classes with our permanent teachers. Simultaneously, my perspective on the seemingly carefree American lifestyle underwent a substantial shift at its core. These encounters left an indelible mark on my understanding of both education and life in the United States.

My deep-seated fascination and profound affection for the United States, a place I had only admired from afar, found its most touching and tangible expression through the presence of two extraordinary individuals. These remarkable educators, who graced the halls of my humble local institution, Kobo Primary School, nestled within the enchanting landscapes of Eastern Hararghe, Ethiopia, unfolded the story of America in my heart, weaving an unbreakable bond that grew stronger with each passing day.

As they shared their knowledge and wisdom, a window to the diverse tapestry of American culture and values was unveiled before my eager eyes. Their passion for teaching and their genuine warmth transcended the physical distance that separated our worlds. It was as if a bridge of understanding and appreciation stretched across continents, connecting our souls.

With every lesson they imparted, every tale they told, and every glimpse into the rich tapestry of America's history and its people, I found myself drawn deeper into the embrace of this remarkable nation. Their dedication to shaping young minds, including mine, not only left an indelible mark on my education but also ignited a flame within me, one that yearned to explore, learn, and connect with the world beyond my homeland.

In their presence, America ceased to be a distant dream; it became a living, breathing entity, fueled by the dreams and aspirations of its people. I am forever grateful for the profound impact these two teachers had on my life, as they illuminated the path that led me to a greater understanding of the world and, ultimately, my own ambitions.

It is after this juncture in life that my mind started to really question things about America. Meeting these two individuals made me admire the United States of America more while acknowledging the idea that America might have its own struggles like all of us.

Chapter six: America the evil nation (The age of Conspiracy theories)

"In a world of conspiracy theories, literature becomes the bulwark against ignorance. Books, like a beacon, illuminate the truth and dispel the darkness of unfounded suspicions." - George Orwell

THE FIRST DECADE OF the new millennium marked a significant period of growth for the printing industry in Ethiopia. I vividly recall the steady stream of newspapers, magazines, and books emerging one after another during those years. It was a time when the publishing landscape thrived, with an abundance of printed materials gracing our shelves.

Indeed, during that era, it seemed like there were distinct seasons in the realm of content. Love stories would captivate our hearts, political narratives would dominate our discussions, and sporting events would grab our attention.

Nevertheless, there was one genre that defied such seasonal fluctuations, standing the test of time throughout that entire decade. It's worth noting, though, that this enduring genre began to wane after 2010, as the digital revolution began to sweep across the landscape, reshaping the way we consumed content.

During that remarkable decade, the conspiracy theory genre in Ethiopia held a unique position. For Ethiopian readers, it wasn't merely conspiracy; it was regarded as a powerful exposé, shedding light on what they perceived as a global web of deception. In their eyes, these narratives weren't fanciful tales but a stark reflection of their own reality.

The core theme of these writings revolved around Ethiopia, casting it as the central figure in a cosmic struggle against the forces of a sinister America, bolstered by European allies. The focus on Ethiopia alone was striking, as it set this genre apart from the global conspiracy narratives that often-encompassed multiple nations. Believe me this is not like a fiction or a movie kind of belief it is a real profound belief by a significant proportion of the society.

Many of these works were authored by individuals who adamantly refused to accept the end of the Ethiopian imperial regime. They clung to a belief that this ancient institution had roots deep in history, transcending the emergence of modern nation-states. Their unwavering commitment to this ideal persisted despite the sweeping changes that had reshaped Ethiopia's political landscape over the past 100 years.

In their pursuit of preserving the imperial legacy, these writers remained staunchly resistant to acknowledging the diversity that defined Ethiopia. They advocated for a vision of the nation that emphasized a single language and a solitary religion. This vision, reminiscent of colonial-era notions, seemed impervious to the passage of time, as if it were frozen in a bygone era.

The persistence of such ideas among a segment of Ethiopian society was indeed remarkable. It was as though they had taken a page from a British playbook from a century ago and held onto it, despite the transformations, challenges, and progress that had shaped their nation. The resilience of these beliefs in the face of evolving times remains a subject of fascination.

For these individuals, principles like globalization, democracy, world trade, international organizations, diplomatic relations, foreign direct investment (FDI), modern education, religious diversity, the philosophical musings of eminent thinkers, and any form of intellectual evolution, be it in the realms of science or art, were all interwoven in a grand conspiracy aimed at undermining the great nation of Ethiopia.

In their eyes, these principles and institutions, which are often seen as essential facets of a modern, interconnected world, were viewed with skepticism and suspicion. Instead of embracing the benefits of globalization or participating in the global community, they perceived these concepts as insidious forces that threatened Ethiopia's sovereignty and cultural identity.

The literature produced by this group mirrored their beliefs, with titles like 'The Satanic Goal in Ethiopia' and 'The Scientific Secret of 666.' These titles try very hard to reflect not only a sense of alarm but also a conviction that Ethiopia was under siege from hidden, malevolent forces.

These works delved into elaborate conspiracies, attempting to connect seemingly unrelated events, concepts, and ideologies to a dark and overarching plot against Ethiopia. They saw the hand of sinister forces at work in every corner of the world and particularly in America, all converging on their beloved nation.

It's remarkable how these writings served as a lens through which this group interpreted the complexities of the modern world. They painted a picture of Ethiopia as a beleaguered nation, standing against a vast and intricate conspiracy designed to erode its uniqueness and resilience.

Despite the vast array of evidence to the contrary, these individuals remained steadfast in their conviction, viewing Ethiopia as a bastion against a global plot of unprecedented scale. These publications created a very skewed view about America for the readers while the common practice of gossiping made those stories trickle to the majority of the population gradually. Just like when we were kids trying to retell movies, adults also retell most of the stories from the publications picturing America as an evil conspirator in their own way creating different kind of incidents of their own.

Books bearing titles that directly implicate Protestant Christians as co-conspirators of the Western world craft a compelling narrative in which Ethiopia assumes a role of exceptional significance. In this vivid portrayal, Ethiopia transcends being merely a nation; it becomes a symbol of untarnished purity, a timeless virgin nation untouched by the winds of change. Picture in mind Israel from the Bible and that is how most of these publications portray Ethiopia.

In contrast, the United States features prominently as the principal malefactor in this narrative—a colossal culprit orchestrating a grand design to erode and corrupt Ethiopia's social fabric. These books assert that the primary mission of the U.S. and its allies is to dismantle Ethiopia's cherished values and traditions. Their objective is to supplant them with an alternative community, one marked by the worship of Lucifer, a malevolent and satanic figure.

The inclusion of Lucifer as a central antagonist adds a dramatic and almost mythical dimension to this narrative. These publications attest that every religious awakening, whether through scripture or any other means, is automatically attributed to American influence.

As an example, the Protestant religion was colloquially dubbed as the 'Wheat Religion,' in most of these publications and day to day communications; a term that drew a connection to the wheat grain shipments from the United States facilitated by USAID for those in need of food assistance.

In Ethiopia, a nation grappling with pervasive poverty and recurring bouts of drought and climate shocks, the sight of wheat sacks and a can of cooking oil bearing the US flag was a commonplace occurrence. Throughout the country, these iconic sacks symbolized a lifeline for millions, as they depended on the aid of US grain just to survive for another day.

HOWEVER, WHAT STRIKES a chord of hypocrisy among these conspiracy genre writers is their inability or reluctance to extend a helping hand, even a loaf of bread or a single penny, while they vehemently criticize the United States for its life-saving wheat aid. In their narratives, they propagate a belief that the US is sending food aid not out of humanitarian intent but as a calculated effort to undermine their religion and promote Protestantism.

This perspective might be rooted in historical context. European and American missionaries played a significant role in the expansion of the Protestant religion, particularly in the western and southern regions of Ethiopia. The memory of foreign missionaries actively working to promote a different religious faith fueled suspicion and conspiracy theories regarding the intentions behind humanitarian aid efforts.

The shared sentiment among teenagers, including myself, during those years was the belief that the United States harbored ulterior motives to weaken our mighty nation, Ethiopia, through the use of religion, coupled with their wheat support. This perception was deeply ingrained, and I vividly recall instances that reflected this sentiment.

One memorable incident involved a church priest from the Orthodox Church who, unreservedly and over an open microphone, openly chastised Protestant followers in our town. His words were harsh and laced with disdain, underlining the divisions and tensions that existed between the two religious' groups. I remember bullying our friends belonging to protestant church as an alien American sympathizer.

Reflecting on those times, we, as teenagers, were not immune to these tensions. We, too, engaged in name-calling and derogatory terms, often labeling children from Protestant families as adherents of the "US Wheat Religion." This term had become commonplace among families and religious leaders, and it continued to signify Protestantism in a nation with a Protestant population numbering more than 20 million today.

From our perspective as children, the arrival of grain from the United States wasn't viewed as a benevolent act aimed at saving lives. Instead, it was perceived as a covert attempt to undermine the rich and distinct culture and religion of Ethiopians, something we held dear.

It's important to underscore that this perception was widespread and deeply ingrained. Many of us harbored the belief that the US had motivations beyond simple humanitarianism. There was a pervasive suspicion that the intention was to erode the cultural and religious fabric of Ethiopia, replacing it with foreign influences.

Some also believed that the American assistance might be a deliberate strategy by the US to create an aid-dependent third-world country, potentially to bolster its declining agriculture sector. This suspicion added a layer of complexity to the way we viewed international aid efforts and their impact on our nation's economy and identity.

Another prevailing belief among some was that US Presidents held not just the highest office in the land but also occupied high-ranking positions within the secretive Illuminati organization. According to this belief, it extended far beyond the political sphere. Musicians, actors, politicians, and even leaders of international organizations were all suspected of being part of this clandestine group, except in rare and exceptional circumstances.

What was most astonishing was the assertion that not only were these exceptional individuals that cannot be members of Illuminati were all from Ethiopia, but they also belonged to the Orthodox Church. It was a narrative that painted a sweeping canvas of intrigue.

I distinctly recall encountering books and magazines that attempted to unravel the mystery. They presented various images of influential global leaders, politicians, and celebrities, scrutinizing them for secret signs and symbols that were interpreted as a covert Morse code, signaling allegiance to the Illuminati.

These publications delved into elaborate theories, connecting seemingly unrelated events and gestures to build a case for the existence of a global conspiracy. They wove a complex tapestry of suspicion and intrigue, shaping perceptions about the influence of the Illuminati on the world's most prominent figures.

A peculiar belief held sway among some that the hand gestures made by US Presidents concealed a secret code, reminiscent of a military cipher from World War I. These signals, it was alleged, held a connection to a broader and sinister satanic objective, invariably linked to the one and only Ethiopia.

What made this belief all the more intriguing was the effort expended in decoding these signs and connecting them to a malevolent conspiracy. In these narratives, Ethiopia often found itself at the center of a grand and ominous design.

It's worth noting that even if one were to stumble upon a photograph featuring similar hand signs made by an Ethiopian Orthodox priest or a prominent figure, the community's response was peculiarly different. Within this framework, individuals from Ethiopia, especially those who belonged to the Orthodox Church, were seemingly exempt from any association with the Illuminati, regardless of their profession or background.

This selective perspective underscored a unique aspect of this belief system — a protective barrier around those considered "one of us." It added a layer of complexity to the conspiracy theories, highlighting the nuanced ways in which individuals interpreted and selectively applied their suspicions to different members of their own community and those outside it.

During this particular era of the century, conversations about America were overwhelmingly dominated by the pervasive belief in the sinister and conspiratorial behavior of its leaders and its people.

For many of us, it seemed as though the United States was continually plotting against our nation, employing various covert mechanisms to undermine our interests. It wasn't uncommon to find individuals who genuinely believed that Satan himself had established his headquarters within the confines of the US. The emergence of issues like legalizing homosexuality and abortion in the United States of America further fueled the satanic view of America in the general public spearheaded by these writers.

For the authors of those books and articles, their motivation may be lay in a deep sense of legacy tied to their monarchical empire. Their writings were driven by a passionate desire to preserve their cultural identity — their language, religion, and values. It was a quest to safeguard what they held dear in the face of perceived external threats.

These narratives might reveal the intricate interplay of fear, identity, and nationalism during that period. They also provide insight into how, the United States, were often portrayed as antagonists of global influence in the eyes of a segment of the Ethiopian population.

Indeed, for many readers, the narratives presented in those books were not perceived as mere fiction but as unassailable facts. In their eyes, it was a stark binary: an evil America pitted against the self-proclaimed holy land and righteous nation of Ethiopia.

What's particularly remarkable is the enduring legacy of these books. Despite the onset of the digital revolution, spearheaded by the rise of social media and digital content, these printed works have managed to withstand the test of time in Ethiopia. They've not only endured but have continued to thrive within the realm of the printing business.

Books like "The Satanic Goal in Ethiopia" have maintained their relevance and continue to be reprinted and republished, often expanding into series. These works have managed to capture and retain the attention of readers, serving as a powerful testament to the influence of conspiracy theories in shaping collective perspectives about America.

Once upon a time, I, too, found myself entangled in the belief that America was a conniving evil conspirator, collaborating with sinister forces to usher in a malevolent new world order. This perception still resonates among many in Ethiopia, who harbor a deep-seated conviction that America is secretly developing technologies to exert control over all of us, ultimately subjecting us to a satanic rule.

It's not uncommon for people to speculate that the Covid-19 pandemic was engineered as a weapon, with vaccines serving as a means of insidious mind control. The idea of a microchip implanted in individuals being the dreaded 666 symbols, a mark of submission to Satan, has also gained traction within this narrative.

In addition to these individual theories, there exists a broader and more encompassing conspiracy, one led by influential international organizations such as the IMF, World Bank, WTO, and various UN agencies. This overarching narrative centers around the United States, casting it as a central player in a global scheme.

This book doesn't aim to provide an intellectual analysis of what America represents, and I won't delve into the intricate details of how the IMF and World Bank's structural adjustment programs have affected developing countries like Ethiopia from a political economy perspective. Instead, I'll focus on describing the perceptions we, as individuals and communities, hold about these institutions, devoid of the lens of formal economics education.

In the eyes of many, these organizations, including the WTO, World Bank, IMF, and various UN agencies, are often seen as instruments wielded by the Americans. This perception remains deeply ingrained and, in my view, continues to hold true.

These institutions are often viewed not merely as impartial bodies but as instruments of influence, where the United States plays a central role in shaping their policies and actions.

Every decision or announcement emanating from these international institutions is often met with widespread skepticism, viewed as potentially fake, undermining, conspiratorial, and even malevolent by the broader community.

Over the span of decades, governments have skillfully leveraged these community perceptions to serve their own self-serving agendas. When anomalies in the economy or society are pointed out by these institutions, they are frequently rejected outright by the majority of the community. In response, governments often attempt to craft their own narrative, creating a falsified image of social and economic development that counters the assessments made by these organizations.

The underlying reason for this widespread rejection of international institutions can be traced back to their association with the United States. Over time, people have developed a propensity to associate conspiracy theories with America, often linking it to sinister or malevolent intentions. This tendency has led to a perception that mischief, deception, or even a malevolent agenda is inherently connected to the United States, which, in turn, shapes how the broader community views these institutions and their pronouncements.

With more and more information being consumed America has now fell down the ladder of being the Christian emblem to a satanic flag bearer conspiring to undermine the just and Godly world order using its evil and demonic techniques.

Chapter seven: America, The Promised Land (DV Lottery)

"With old age comes great understanding"
- Me

AGE, INDEED, HAS A remarkable way of imparting wisdom, often surpassing the significance of the sheer volume of information one accumulates. As I've grown older, I've found myself dispelling many of the misconceptions I once held about America. With each passing year, the veil of myth has been lifted, revealing a clearer understanding of what is real and what is not.

As I completed my primary education and embarked on my secondary schooling, America evolved into a distant dreamland, a place I aspired to visit someday. It was during this period that I first learned about the Diversity Visa (DV) lottery program. I discovered that nearly every young and adult individual in my local community, who could read and write, harbored the same dream of journeying to the United States and participating in the annual DV lottery program.

Even individuals who hold the belief that the United States is the sinister force behind the destruction of their beloved Ethiopia, orchestrating a malicious global agenda, are willing to make incredible sacrifices to relocate to the US and start a new chapter in their lives. It's quite ironic, isn't it?

The Diversity Visa (DV) lottery program continues to hold immense significance in Ethiopia to this day. I can vividly recall instances when a fortunate individual secured the coveted lottery win, and the entire community would come together to celebrate it as if it were a grand wedding or a birthday extravaganza.

Much like the annual holidays that bring joy throughout the country, the announcement of the DV lottery used to be eagerly awaited with great enthusiasm and cheer. It's a testament to the enduring allure and hope that America represents to many Ethiopians, transcending even the most deeply held beliefs and skepticism about its intentions.

In the old days, the only pathway to enter the Diversity Visa (DV) lottery program was by sending applications through the post office. As soon as the application season was announced, people would eagerly form lines, each step taking them closer to what they saw as the promised land. I recognize that this may sound perplexing and contradictory: portraying America as a promised land for a people who, at times, regarded it as an antagonist. However, I won't offer you the oversimplified notion that they sought to either redeem or liberate America from its perceived evils. The truth is far more intricate; it's a perplexing conundrum.

Practically speaking, even those who considered America as an adversary saw it as a promised land of sorts. It was a paradoxical perspective that prevailed. Almost everyone aspired to make the journey to the United States, despite any reservations about its intentions. I recall the various schemes and strategies that emerged during the announcement of DV lottery winners, highlighting the extent to which the American dream resonated within our Ethiopian community.

It's a testament to the allure of the American dream that some individuals went to extraordinary lengths. There were instances where natural siblings, bound by the shared aspiration of moving to the United States, made the unconventional decision to enter into marriages of convenience. These unions which were considered to be immoral and unjust by the whole community were out of a practical necessity to accompany their DV lottery-winning family member to the promised land of the United States.

In some of the most dedicated cases, one partner might be willing to invest a substantial amount of money to secure a marriage with a stranger, who had emerged victorious in the DV lottery. It was a unique manifestation of determination and commitment to their collective goal of starting a new life in the US. This phenomenon reveals the profound impact that the promise of America had on individuals and families in Ethiopia.

The willingness to enter into such arrangements was a reflection of the widespread desire for the opportunities and possibilities that

America represented. It was a symbol of hope and a chance for a better future, one that many were prepared to pursue at any cost possible.

The allure of going to the United States was perceived as a shortcut to a better life, a path that virtually everyone pursued with little understanding of the challenges and sacrifices required to succeed in the US. Whether one was a student with dreams of pursuing higher education, a trader seeking new opportunities, a civil servant yearning for a fresh start, a doctor contemplating a thriving practice, or even those who were already considered very successful in their fields here in Ethiopia, all shared a common aspiration: to enroll in the Diversity Visa (DV) lottery program with the hope of securing their ticket to America.

It's fascinating how the American dream had the power to captivate individuals from diverse backgrounds and professions. The promise of America represented a beacon of hope, a chance to escape the limitations and uncertainties of their current circumstances. Despite the varied paths they had walked in Ethiopia, the pursuit of the DV lottery united them in their shared desire for a brighter future in the United States.

The decision to enter the DV lottery was, in many ways, a testament to the enduring belief in the opportunities and possibilities that America offered. It was a collective dream, a journey undertaken by countless individuals, each with their unique story and motivation. The pursuit of the American dream was a unifying force that transcended differences and brought together people from all walks of life, bound by the shared hope of making it in the land of opportunity.

I can vividly recall those moments when some of us, who hadn't been fortunate enough to be selected in the Diversity Visa (DV) lottery, would resort to insults directed at those who had won the opportunity to relocate to the United States. It was not uncommon for harsh words to be exchanged, with derogatory terms like "bathroom cleaners" hurled at those who had secured their spot in the program.

The envy and frustration among those left behind were palpable. If you happened to mention to a neighbor or acquaintance that someone you knew, perhaps even a member of your own family, had been fortunate in the DV lottery and had moved to the US, you could almost guarantee that a snide comment was coming your way. The retort would often be along the lines of, "Oh, so they're off to clean bathroom toilets now, are they?"

It was a sharp, biting response fueled by jealousy and, to some extent, a coping mechanism for those who had not been selected. In a peculiar way, it was a defense mechanism against the disappointment of not winning the coveted lottery. The label of "bathroom cleaner" became a symbol of resentment, encapsulating the complex emotions that the DV program stirred within our community.

Looking back, it's a testament to the emotional rollercoaster that the DV lottery represented for so many Ethiopians. It was a source of hope and aspiration for some, while for others, it was a bitter reminder of missed opportunities. The use of such derogatory terms was a stark reflection of the intense desire and frustration that surrounded the pursuit of the American dream, even if it meant resorting to harsh words in moments of disappointment.

Even though I can't say for certain, it was a prevailing belief among many of us that migrants who had the opportunity to move to the United States through the Diversity Visa (DV) program would often end up working as bathroom cleaners, regardless of their educational backgrounds, which could even include doctors.

The intriguing part of this perception was that, at that stage, most people regarded America as the ultimate powerhouse for economic freedom. It was seen as a land of boundless opportunities, where one could potentially achieve their dreams. However, the notion that highly educated individuals, including doctors, might find themselves in roles like bathroom cleaning was a paradox that persisted in our collective imagination.

IN ESSENCE, THIS DICHOTOMY encapsulated the complex mix of hope and uncertainty that characterized our views of America at the time. It was a place of aspiration, yet also a place where the path to success seemed anything but straightforward. The juxtaposition of these beliefs highlighted the multifaceted nature of our collective perception of the United States as both a land of opportunity and a place where challenges and misconceptions coexisted.

There was also the peculiar phenomenon that many individuals from Ethiopia sought American citizenship by claiming political persecution in their homeland. For me, it often felt like a scam perpetrated on the American government, and I held a skeptical view of such cases. My skepticism, however, did not deny the grim reality that Ethiopia ranked among the most dangerous places in the world to engage in political activities. Here, people could face prosecution or even the gravest consequences for merely holding an alternative political viewpoint or expressing their unique interests.

Nevertheless, I couldn't help but harbor doubts about the true motivations behind those Ethiopians seeking asylum in the United States. In my perspective, the quest for political freedom was often secondary, if not entirely incidental. The primary objective for the majority of asylum seekers venturing to the US was rooted in the pursuit of economic freedom. Political asylum, in their eyes, served as a means to an end, and that end was economic liberation.

The United States represented the ultimate gateway to ascend the socioeconomic hierarchy within Ethiopian society at this stage of my life and beyond to this date in my life. It was seen as the land of opportunity, where individuals could transcend the limitations they faced back in Ethiopia. The pursuit of economic prosperity was the driving force behind many decisions to seek asylum, and the notion of political freedom, while undoubtedly significant, often played second fiddle to the allure of financial security and a better life.

In this intricate tapestry of motivations and aspirations, the desire for economic freedom stood out as a prevailing force. It was a testament to the powerful allure that the United States held for Ethiopians, where dreams of prosperity and a brighter future outweighed the complexities and nuances of their asylum claims. The pursuit of the American dream, in many ways, became synonymous with the pursuit of economic freedom and a chance to climb the ladder of success in Ethiopian society.

I distinctly recall the advice I received about how to go about pursuing the dream of moving to the United States. It was suggested to me that the first step was to obtain an identification card that would align me with an opposition armed political group. Then, the journey involved traveling to neighboring countries, like Kenya, by road and seeking political asylum in the one and only nation of the United States.

It was a well-known fact that numerous individuals identified themselves as political asylum seekers after arriving in the US, often with the primary goal of obtaining a residence permit. The process was not without its complexities and challenges, but the general consensus was that the effort and persistence were entirely justified. The reason for this belief was evident when you observed my town. Those who enjoyed better living conditions, with sturdy roofs above their heads, stylish clothing, and access to good food, were predominantly individuals with relatives settled in the US.

The hustle and bustle of pursuing political asylum and navigating the intricate pathways to the United States were seen as a small price to pay for the potential rewards that awaited those who succeeded.

In the end, the pursuit of the American dream, even through unconventional means, became a driving force for many, as it offered the possibility of a better life and prosperity that transcended borders and boundaries.

Even today, the United States continues to be regarded as the most promising pathway out of poverty for countless Ethiopians. The allure of America as a land of opportunity persists, and this dream remains deeply ingrained in the hearts and minds of many.

In the year 2020 alone, more than a million Ethiopian citizens applied for the Diversity Visa (DV) program, according to data from the US State Department. This staggering number underscores the magnitude of the desire for a chance at a better life that America represents. For Ethiopians, going to the US symbolizes not only a personal journey but a transformative experience that can elevate the standard of living for individuals and uplift the quality of life for their families.

The pursuit of the American dream is, for many, a beacon of hope, a chance to break free from the cycle of poverty and reach for prosperity. It's a testament to the enduring belief in the opportunities and possibilities that America offers. The idea that one can change not only their own standard of living but also positively impact their family's standard of life by making the journey to the US is a powerful motivator. It's a dream that transcends generations and continues to inspire Ethiopians to strive for a brighter future in the land of opportunity.

However, It's also a reality that often goes unnoticed by the locals—the sacrifices and challenges faced by those who immigrate to the United States. There is an unspoken, yet deeply ingrained, expectation within the community that these individuals will send back substantial sums of money. In the eyes of many, an immigrant who makes the journey to the US and does not contribute funds for building their parents' house or investing in other life-changing endeavors would be viewed as a source of disgrace to their family.

The weight of these expectations can be overwhelming. Immigrants are not only pursuing their American dream but are also entrusted with the hopes and aspirations of their loved ones back home. They carry the burden of not only improving their own lives but also contributing to the betterment of their families.

It's a complex dynamic where the pursuit of personal success is inextricably tied to familial obligations. For many, the American dream is not just an individual endeavor but a collective one, where the achievement of one member reflects on the entire family. The pressure to meet these expectations can be immense, and it underscores the sacrifices and struggles that often go unnoticed by the local community.

In general, it's a testament to the profound sense of responsibility and duty that drives immigrants to succeed, not only for themselves but also for their families. The desire to uplift their loved ones and fulfill the hopes placed upon them is a powerful motivator, even if it comes with its own set of challenges and sacrifices.

The notion of America as a land of opportunity becomes firmly etched in the minds of nearly every high school student. It's a belief that takes root early in life, often influenced by stories of success and the promise of boundless potential that the United States represents.

In high schools across Ethiopia, young minds are engrossed with the idea that America is a place where dreams can be realized, where hard work and determination can lead to a brighter future. This belief is fostered through education, conversations with peers, and exposure to the stories of those who have ventured to the US in pursuit of their aspirations.

From a young age, students are encouraged to reach for the stars and consider the possibilities that await them in the land of opportunity, a belief that can shape their ambitions and aspirations for years to come.

I have a vivid memory of a local movie that delved into this very issue. The film featured a central character who was ailing and had been referred by the hospital's medical board to seek treatment in the United States. What followed was a captivating storyline, akin to a competitive bidding process, where various caretakers vied for the opportunity to accompany the ailing individual to the US. Each participant had to meet certain criteria, including providing a substantial cash investment, a requirement that played into the desire to tap into the fervent aspiration of people yearning for a chance to go to America.

In the movie, the friends of the ailing man embarked on an elaborate selection process, meticulously evaluating the potential caretakers. This process wasn't just about choosing someone to accompany their sick friend; it was also about capitalizing on the high demand among people eager to make their way to America. The cash investment, intended to cover the expenses of the caretaker's journey, became a focal point in this elaborate scheme.

The movie comically captured the complexities and intricacies surrounding the pursuit of the American dream, even in the context of a fictional narrative. It highlighted the lengths to which individuals would go to secure an opportunity to make the journey to the US. The story, in many ways, mirrored the real-life aspirations and challenges faced by many Ethiopians as they strive to reach the land of opportunity.

The allure of the caretaker visa, once stamped in one's passport, held the tantalizing promise that the individual could explore various avenues to remain in the United States indefinitely, effectively making a life in the longed-for promised land. It was a beacon of hope, a potential escape from the homeland's challenges, and an opportunity to secure a brighter future on American soil.

The movie that explored this theme was a comedy, designed to entertain while shedding light on the very real social issue ingrained in the local culture—the insatiable desire of the people to make their way to the US, regardless of the sacrifices involved. It playfully mocked the lengths to which individuals would go, and the elaborate schemes they would devise, all in pursuit of the American dream.

The stark reality is that the aspiration to move to America through various means is a genuine and prevalent phenomenon. People are willing to pay exorbitant financial and personal costs to chase this dream.

I've only mentioned one such movie here, but it's worth noting that there seems to be a distinct sub-genre of films that squarely focus on the theme of people's aspirations to reach America. These movies delve into the complex narratives of individuals struggling to achieve their dreams on American soil. While the movie I previously mentioned is a comedy, offering a satirical take on the pursuit of the American dream, there are many others that tackle this subject with a more serious tone.

One such movie is even rumored to have been written by the current Ethiopian Prime Minister. This particular film takes a different path, as it leans towards tragedy, shedding light on the harsh realities of illegal immigration. It doesn't shy away from portraying the ugly truth of the perils that many face when attempting to reach the United States. Despite the somber tone, the overarching goal remains the same—reaching the mighty USA.

These movies, whether comedic or tragic, serve as reflections of the deep-rooted desires and struggles of Ethiopians who yearn for a better life in America. They capture the multifaceted nature of this journey, highlighting the diverse experiences, challenges, and emotions that come with the pursuit of the American dream. Whether through humor or tragedy, these films offer a window into the enduring allure of the United States and the lengths individuals are willing to go to in order to make it to the land of opportunity.

From Ethiopia, only a handful have managed to achieve the dream of reaching the promised land, the United States. Yet, for some peculiar reason, I observed that many of those who successfully made their way to the US exhibited rather unusual behavior upon their return.

It was noticeable that the members of the diaspora who had spent time in the US often displayed traits that were, at times, challenging for the locals to comprehend. There was a noticeable shift in their demeanor—some became more arrogant, seemingly entitled, and occasionally displayed rudeness, adopting a self-serving attitude that was quite different from their previous interactions with the community.

This transformation, though not universal, was evident enough to become a subject of discussion within the community. It was as if the experience of living in the United States had a profound impact on their behavior, sometimes leading to a disconnection from their roots and a sense of detachment from the local culture.

When a member of the diaspora returns from America, it's often noticeable that they immediately exhibit behaviors that can be perceived as socially unconventional. There's a transformation that occurs, particularly among those returning from the United States, which is quite distinct.

One of the most apparent changes is a discerning attitude towards food, with returning diaspora members often becoming selective in their culinary preferences. They may develop a sense of being part of a high-class echelon, creating an air of untouchable sophistication. These shifts may also extend to language, as they might introduce new dialects and pronunciations to the local language, showcasing a very unique way of speaking, walking, and even eating.

The impact of their time spent in America is often reflected in their attire, with a penchant for jewelry, branded clothing, and flashy materials. These outward signs of prosperity become direct implications of their return from the United States.

However, what remains perplexing is the underlying cause of the perceived arrogance among some returning diaspora members. While they may accumulate material possessions, it's challenging to comprehend the root of the shift in their demeanor towards the local community. The transformation goes beyond external appearances and material wealth, and a deeper impact of their experiences abroad that shapes their interactions and attitudes upon their return.

However, what's remarkable is that these ill behaviors are often accepted without question locally if that individual is returning from the United States.

The underlying reason for this acceptance may be rooted in the perception of America as a unique nation, one that is held in high regard by many. There is a prevailing sentiment that anyone who has had the opportunity to go to the US and return should be granted some latitude for their sometimes-eccentric behavior. It's as if the mere act of setting foot in America bestows a certain status that exempts individuals from scrutiny.

In this context, getting married to an American diaspora is considered a significant achievement, perhaps the greatest accomplishment locally. The allure of marrying someone who has spent time in the United States is so strong that some women end up in unions with American diaspora individuals they have never met in person, culminating in lavish and extravagant wedding celebrations. It's become a sort of status symbol, and the fancier and more luxurious the wedding, the higher the probability that it involves someone who has returned from America.

So, at one point in my life for me and most of us back here in Ethiopia America became the promised land. Onto the land of opportunity where milk and honey flows!!!!!!!!!!!!

Chapter eight:
Enlightenment

"Enlightenment is man's emergence from his self-imposed immaturity. Immaturity is the inability to use one's understanding without guidance from another. This immaturity is self-imposed when its cause lies not in a lack of understanding but in a lack of resolve and courage to use it without guidance from another."
- Immanuel Kant

Between the years I spent in high school and college, I underwent a personal journey of growth and maturation in my understanding of America or anything for that matter. This transformation was sparked by a variety of factors, from the movies I watched to the books I read, and it marked a very significant evolution in my perceptions.

During this pivotal period, I began to engage with American culture and society in a more profound way. The films I watched offered insights into different aspects of American life, from its diverse communities to its rich history to its complex tapestry.

As I delved deeper into these cultural resources, my understanding of America evolved for the better and worse. I started to appreciate and truly view the nuances of its society, its strengths, and its challenges. It was a journey of discovery that broadened my perspective and allowed me to see America in a more balanced light than ever.

This period marked a crucial phase in my journey of understanding America. It was during these years, as I progressed from high school to college, that I gained a deeper insight into the complexities of the United States. My evolving comprehension extended beyond the mythical, unbalanced, and fairy tale liked impressions I had previously held.

It was during this time that I began to discern where the complexities and challenges lay within America, and where they did not. I embarked on a journey of enlightenment. I delved into the historical events surrounding America's wars in places like Vietnam, Somalia, Iraq, and Afghanistan.

I realized that the United States, like any nation, had its moments of both commendable actions and questionable decisions. This newfound awareness allowed me to approach discussions about America's role in the world with a more informed perspective.

During this period, my cinematic preferences took a significant turn. I transitioned from primarily watching action-packed movies and curated happy go lucky middle eastern satellite televisions censored

Hollywood movies to exploring the works of acclaimed actors like Denzel Washington, Meryl Streep, Tom Hanks, and many others. It marked a phase where I expanded my cinematic horizons beyond the adrenaline-filled plots. But more it was an eye opening point in my self-discovery defining America as an outsider always amazed by the very architecture of this mighty nation.

I found myself drawn to a different genre of movies, particularly romantic comedies, historical dramas, and other dramas from Hollywood. Those movies showing the real challenges every day Americans face daily in their life turned the tides away for my long-held viewpoints about America.

During this period, my perception of America underwent a profound transformation. I began to see it not only as the most powerful nation on the global stage but also as a nation with its own vulnerabilities and complexities. It was a realization that added layers of depth to my understanding of this influential country.

By this time, I had become well-acquainted with English as a language, and this linguistic proficiency allowed me to connect more deeply with the emotions and actions portrayed in movies. I started to discern the subtle nuances in storytelling. Furthermore, the news began to make sense to me as I tuned into channels like CNN, BBC, and Al Jazeera, which introduced me to a more nuanced and multifaceted view of America, beyond what I had seen in movies.

Yet, the most transformative agent during this period was undoubtedly the rise of social media and the internet. These technological advancements reshaped not only my perspective but also the outlook of many around the world. They provided unprecedented access to information, allowing us to explore diverse viewpoints, engage with global events in real-time, and connect with people from all walks of life.

It was during this time that I personally came to realize the true greatness and flaws of the United States of America. I began to appreciate its strengths and accomplishments, recognizing the enduring impact it had on the world stage. However, I also became more aware of its imperfections, acknowledging the challenges and complexities that existed within the nation.

This phase in my journey of understanding America marked a turning point, where my perception evolved from one based primarily on cinematic portrayals to a more comprehensive and nuanced view of the nation. It was a time of awakening, where I embraced the real complexities of America.

I started to learn about the beauty of American democracy and the foundations that makeup this great nation. It is maybe the time a rather funny looking viewpoints I had about America started to fade away and a more serious and balanced view started to emerge. You might have noticed the shift in the chapter itself since I am talking CNN and BBC things have taken a turn.

It's worth noting that movies still continued to play a pivotal role in my ongoing education and exploration about America sitting thousands of miles away in East Africa. Through cinematic portrayals, I learned about significant figures like Abraham Lincoln and his remarkable deeds, which left an indelible mark on the nation's history. I remember the day I watched the 2012 biography Lincoln. The movie left a lasting impact on my complex view about America. The story of Lincoln portrayed in that movie was sort of a miracle happening in front of you just like it is from the Bible. I don't know whether that version of the movie is over dramatized or not, but my innocent views of Americas greatness and myth just became true in a very different manner. It was one movie that lamented America as the one and only great nation in my mind characterized by a collection of great minds.

Conversely, my newfound fascination with these certain movie genres made me delve into the darker chapters of American history, discovering the shameful aspects that had marred the nation's past. These included the haunting legacy of slavery, the deep scars of racial discrimination, the ugliness of hate, the grip of greed, the turmoil of the Civil War, and a myriad of other flaws that had shaped America's history. We all studied the brutality of European colonialists since it was an African issue but there was no lesson about American history in our books as far as I remember. So, learning about this flaws about America was earth shattering revelation.

This dual exploration, through cinema and literature, allowed me to confront the complexities of America's past. It was an education that did not shy away from the painful truths but instead encouraged a deeper understanding of the nation's journey, with all its triumphs and tragedies. These lessons became part of my broader comprehension of America as a multifaceted nation with a rich and tumultuous history, where the narratives of greatness and imperfection were intertwined just like any nation on earth.

During this period, I had a profound realization that America, as a nation, is a tapestry woven from a multitude of diverse peoples. It was a time when I began to discover the different tapestry of American society.

The discovery of this mosaic was nothing short of revelatory. While I am still in Ethiopia through the lenses of movies and social media I came across various communities making up this Country of America I am fascinated with, each with its distinct identity and heritage. There were the African Americans, The Jewish community, the Caucasians, Mexicans, Asians, and Native Americans, each bringing their own unique perspectives and experiences to the American story I scripted, narrated, validated and told for ages with my friends.

During this period, I became acutely aware of the disparities and discriminations that existed within this nation of remarkable people. It was a realization that cast a sobering light on the complexities of America, a country where many, including Africans like those from my homeland, aspired to go. It was also a time when I discovered that even within this diverse land, discrimination persisted, affecting Americans who were Black.

The stark contrast between the image of America as a beacon of opportunity and the reality of discrimination faced by Black Americans was a revelation. It was a disheartening reminder that, despite America being considered the promised land of opportunity with flowing honey and milk by many of the people around the world, there remained deep-seated issues related to racial inequality and injustice. The images of police brutality against black individuals and the inherent violence within these black communities were one of the many reasons that led me to rethink about my plight to the promised land.

The series of history lessons I received about America, from movies, magazines, and school, now provides a more accurate depiction of the United States of America. Impacting my viewpoints in a more complex way.

It may have been at this juncture that I came to the profound realization that greatness is not an exclusive attribute of the United States. I began to realize that America was not always as influential and great as it is today, particularly when considering its status a mere century ago. As my perspective broadened, I found myself acknowledging the greatness of numerous nations across different periods, ranging from the ancients to the more recent.

I came to recognize that America's ascent to the position of the world's greatest nation occurred after many other remarkable civilizations, such as Greece, India, China, Egypt, Persia, Rome, and the Ottomans, to name just a few, had previously held that mantle.

One thing that struck me during this time was how my perception of America transformed. It became clear that America wasn't the mythical place I had once imagined. It also became clearer that America was not the promised land me and million others really craved to go to risking it all, especially as a black person. It is may be the time I stopped turning in my DV lottery application as a person. Although, the application process of the DV lottery became easier and easier over the years becoming one click away from a once cumbersome post office application process I refrained from submitting one ever. It was like finding out the promised land with milk and honey flowing turning to be a nightmare place of laying bricks just like the stories of the Jewish people I grow up reading from the bible. For someone who grew up proud of his skin color due to the bravery of his forefathers who fought the white colonialist from Italy at the battle of Adwa and registered the first black people victory over the colonialists it was a very disturbing revelation. Imagining America as a place I can be discriminated for just by my look took a lot to sink in.

I also realized that America, for all its power and influence, wasn't invincible. It hit me that they could face defeat in a conflict against a nation like Somalia, which was disassociated and disintegrated, lacking a central government. This shook my belief in America's invulnerability.

Digging deeper into the pages of history, I uncovered instances where the United States of America got involved in conflicts, like the proxy war in Somalia, using nations like Ethiopia as messengers in the name of peace. It made me see the shades in America's actions on the global stage, showing that things were not as straightforward as I once thought.

It was an eye opening moment when I realized that America could be challenged in battle by some of the world's poorest nations, despite lacking access to advanced military technology and ammunition. Vietnam, a nation with limited resources but unwavering determination, proved that even the most technologically advanced nations could face formidable adversaries. Somalia, the most disorganized nation can torment the mighty United States.

These revelations marked another turning point again in my understanding of America, shaping the way I viewed the nation and its role in the world. It was a personal journey of discovery and a shift in my perspective about the complexities of the real America beyond the myths I had believed in.

My dreamy, almost mythical thoughts about America were shattered when I discovered that it was the US that had trained the Taliban leader, Osama Bin Laden. It was like finding out Santa is not real for me (Just kidding Ethiopians have no idea who Santa is until we started watching Hollywood movies, so it might be like finding out Santa is not real for an American).

Fun Fact: Did you know In Ethiopia we celebrate Christmas in Ethiopia totally different from the rest of the world on January 7th which is in the fourth month of our calendar and there is no Santa at all.

IN WHAT LOOKS LIKE a series of negative history bombings on my mind Learning about the American bombings of Hiroshima and Nagasaki, where nuclear weapons were used, left another profound impact on me. The horrifying causalities from that incident made my stomach sick questioning my American dream a nightmare of a kind. Those compassionate, loving, intelligent, and unlimited positive adjectives represented people I always admired became a symbol of terror in my mind.

Adding on the many complex layers of confusion I already grasped about America, the defeat of the United States and its multinational allies or forces in Lebanon was another event that shook my long-held perceptions. It made me realize that even the mightiest nation could face setbacks in its foreign military operation. For a person who used to believe in America that dissipate any one on earth with ease and zero casualty since childhood it was a sad slap on a face. It is like finding out the Hercules, or the David in my story falling in the hands of the enemy easily. The country which I once thought invincible and indispensable just fell down the ladder of greatness and looked vulnerable.

AS I DELVED DEEPER into events, I uncovered America's infamous involvements in various countries, from Libya and Yemen to Iraq and Afghanistan, among many other military interventions. This continuous revelation of American missteps and mishaps in various parts of the world was like a series of shocks to my long-standing mighty views of the United States of America.

These revelations painted a more complex picture of America's role in the world, far removed from the idealized notions I once held. It was a journey of awakening, where my understanding of America evolved as a response to series of history lessons.

History lessons were like a beacon of light, guiding me towards a more balanced perspective. They illuminated the fact that America was simply one nation among the many others in the world.

It became clear to me that nations like Russia, the United Kingdom, France, Germany, and Canada were equally significant players on the global stage. The world is much more than America and greatness can be found elsewhere other than the United States.

This newfound awareness helped me develop a new window of view into the nations of the world other than America. America, once the center of my whole world, was now part of a much larger mosaic of nations, each with its own story to tell. A story of great and mighty people in addition to a story of ordinary and sloppy people equally.

Simple facts, such as the Ethiopian government's involvement in a mission on behalf of the US to bomb Somalia, left me perplexed about the mightiest nation in the world.

Growing up in my community, we often heard tales of conflicts with Somalis, and the prevailing narrative was that Ethiopia had emerged victorious in those encounters, though I couldn't verify the authenticity of these stories. So, when I discovered that America faced challenges in Somalia, it forced me to reassess the beliefs and narratives I had carried since my early years.

This moment of reflection prompted me to question the assumptions and scripts I had developed about the United States. It was a realization that the world's dynamics were far more intricate than I had once thought.

Movies that portray the civil rights movement in America, such as "Selma," "The Butler," , "Remember the Titans," "The Help," "42," "Loving," "Malcolm X," and others, have provoked deep thought within me about the United States.

These films served as powerful tools for me to reexamine the essence of America time and time again. They depicted the inherent problems and challenges characterizing this mighty nation.

"Selma" transported me to the heart of the civil rights struggle, making me ponder the sacrifices made for justice in a land I thought justice was just a cup of tea the innocents sip easily. "The Butler" unraveled the complex dynamics of race relations and political change over the years in a distant land I always look up to as a land of freedom, equality and democracy. While, "Lincoln" painted a vivid picture of saint like leadership during a time of monumental transformation while making me question the belief I had about America as the land of intelligent people challenged by the antagonists in the movie.

"Remember the Titans" celebrated unity amidst racial tensions, while "The Help" unflinchingly exposed the disparities and injustices that lingered beneath the surface. "42" took me back to a time when baseball became a battleground for civil rights. Giving me a complex understanding into what made America.

The love story of "Loving" highlighted the struggle for interracial marriage, and "Malcolm X" offered an insight into the complex journey of an iconic figure. All of these movies painted a multifaceted picture of America's history, each narrating a chapter of the ongoing journey toward a more just and equitable nation. Not one I once scripted and validated as perfect nation on earth with equality and democracy.

Fun Fact: *Did you know the artist/actress who played Mildred Loving in the 2016 movie Loving was born in Ethiopia.*

The impact of these films, combined with the history lessons I've imbibed, has undeniably crafted a new reality in my understanding of mighty America. They have contributed to my evolving perception of the nation, where its strengths and weaknesses are interwoven in the fabric of its history.

So, America at this point in my life is both great and flawed, the imperfection within that once mighty nation in my mind silently and progressively settled in.

Chapter Nine: Obama Years

"Barack Obama's election as the first African American President of the United States is an inspiration to us all. It shows that dreams, no matter how impossible they may seem, can become reality."
- Nelson Mandela

THE ONLY PERIOD IN history when most of us in Ethiopia, and perhaps the entire continent of Africa, felt an unprecedented connection to the United States of America was may be when a charismatic Black individual embarked on a historic journey to run for the presidency of the greatest nation on Earth in the year 2008. His campaign was marked by a resounding slogan that resonated globally: "YES WE CAN." It was a moment propelled every soul into a state of superior capability engraved in self-confidence.

This charismatic figure captivated the imagination of people not only in America but also across the world, including Africa. His message of hope, unity, and progress transcended borders and touched the hearts of many who had never been interested or not connected to American politics. It was like listening to your favorite sermon preaching bible verses at the church to many ears throughout Ethiopia and the rest of Africa. Even those people who has no idea of what he was talking about cheered for him admiring his captivating charisma. His endearing look while delivering messages in a totally alien language to most of the locals back here in Ethiopia was captivating enough mesmerized by seeing someone looking like them leading the way in one of the greatest nation on earth.

For Americans and western societies, It might be a time when the power of words and the promise of change seemed to bridge the gap between continents. The belief that positive change was possible, embodied in the "YES WE CAN" ethos, reverberated far beyond American shores, fostering a sense of shared optimism and aspiration among people around the world. But, back here in the backyards of Ethiopia it was all about admiration for the best governance system in the world, democracy, and the great people representing it proudly. So, as far as Ethiopia is considered it was not about his message or his policy it was all about seeing a black guy making it to the top of the world. And maybe that was true for most of Africans too.

I can still vividly recall the extraordinary level of excitement that permeated my locality during the Obama presidency. It was a time when people couldn't stop talking about it, and conversations about this historic moment seemed to echo everywhere, from the bustling streets to the quiet corners of our community. Radio programs and TV shows in local language were fully captivated by the news of this black guys campaign for the highest office in the free world. Teachers tend to frequently give examples in classes referencing Obama while teaching us democracy in Civics classes.

The enthusiasm was intense, and discussions about President Obama's leadership and the promise of his presidency were pervasive. It was as if his election had ignited a collective spark of hope and optimism that transcended the boundaries of our local community. The politically silent and dormant society found a totally separate space to rejoice about away from its own disengaged political space.

The historic significance of the moment, with the first Black president of the United States taking office, resonated deeply with people around the world. In the lead-up to the historic presidency of Barack Obama, news outlets like CNN, BBC, and Al Jazeera had us all riveted to our seats. It was a period of intense political interest in Ethiopia, and these international news sources played a pivotal role in keeping us informed and engaged. The only time I think Ethiopians are that much engaged in politics might be when there is a very significant violent political revolution happening every decade or two.

Many of us followed the primary elections and the final presidential race as if they were unfolding right here in our own country. The excitement was palpable, and it seemed as if the entire nation was collectively holding its breath, eagerly awaiting the outcome.

What stood out was the universal support and enthusiasm for this charismatic Black candidate. People from all walks of life openly rooted for him to succeed. It was a time when the boundaries of nations seemed to blur, and the representation embodied by Barack Obama's candidacy resonated with people across Africa.

It is important to know that all of the people rooting for Obama at the time of his campaign never know what his policies were. I remember a lot of people regretting supporting Obama after they came to know his stances on homosexuality, abortion and other liberal rights advocated by the democrats in the United States of America. Later in Obamas presidency the local Ethiopians like me who totally forgot about Americas conspirator satanic mission after finding some one like us at the helm of the free world immediately woke up and realized he is way far from Ethiopians who are conservative religious Christians and Muslims all across the nation.

DURING THE 2008 ELECTIONS local TV stations in Ethiopia, all of which were controlled by the state, provided extensive coverage of the American election process unlike any time before. It was as if they were bringing the unfolding events directly to our own country. This level of coverage was nothing short of extraordinary and had a profound impact on us. For Ethiopians who had never seen any body they call ours representing them on political arena covered on Tv this was very new.

For those of us in Ethiopia, it felt like we were watching a nostalgic movie or living in a fantasy world. The reason for this was rooted in the stark contrast between the American election and the political system that prevailed in Ethiopia at the time. Our own political landscape was characterized by repression, authoritarianism, and a tightly closed system. For instance, while growing up, the top political leaders in the country I know from TV led the country for more than 20 years all came into the nation politics using fire arms. So to put it very simply, a bunch of militants busted the sitting government and told everyone from now on they are the ones running everyone's life for worse. And they stayed there for about thirty years which is about my age and some violent revolution again busted them giving the people another face.

So, for many of us, the American election was not just a distant event; it was a symbol of hope and aspiration, a glimpse into what a more open and democratic political system could look like. It underscored the importance of the values of transparency, freedom, and democracy, which we longed for in our own country generation after generation.

As a citizen living in one of the poorest third-world countries, I, like many others, had never witnessed a government elected or a representative in power who truly belonged to or resembled the ordinary people. In our context, democracy often felt like nothing more than a slogan taught in classrooms, a tool that the government used to maintain its grip on power. It was a concept that seemed distant and detached from our everyday lives.

For most of us, democracy had become synonymous with political propaganda, a message that was disseminated by those in power to maintain their control. The reality we faced was one of limited political representation, where the voices of the ordinary people often went unheard. The different terms in democracy often used sounded like representation of autocracy and repression for Ethiopians. Being a member of an opposition political party is a taboo concept most of our parents worked relentlessly to guide us away from it.

However, amidst this backdrop, something extraordinary happened. We were treated to a spectacle that felt like a miracle—an individual who seemed just like us, someone who hailed from humble beginnings (well that is just being a black African American for us), was courageously battling it out for the highest office in the world. The democratic process unfolded in the most dramatic and transparent fashion, in stark contrast to the political landscape we were accustomed to.

This remarkable experience opened our eyes to the true potential of democracy or American democracy in this case. It was a reminder that democracy could be more than just a hollow promise if it is in the greatest country of all; it could be a tangible force for change and a vehicle for the voices of ordinary citizens to be heard on a global stage when it is in America. It was a moment of hope and inspiration, offering a glimpse of what could be achieved when the principles of democracy were upheld and embraced in their true spirit. While, the collection of all this was all about magnifying America in the minds of everyone across my locality. It was like a miraculous balancing sort of a thing making most of us again yearn to go to the United States. The many wounds that crushed our dream about the promised land were cured by the greatness of American democracy.

Some of the amusing memories that still linger involve the playful way in which people jokingly associated Barack Obama with being one of our own (I meant literally our own). Not just Kenyan, but even in my native Oromo language, there exists a common name, 'Aboma,' which translates to something akin to a commander or a leader. It was during this time that some folks humorously argued that the man's name should be 'Aboma,' not 'Obama,' and that it was the pronunciation by the white folks that led to the 'Obama' version.

This playful twist on his name became a source of light-hearted banter and jest. People playfully debated whether 'Aboma' was the correct name all along, and it was just a matter of pronunciation that led to the now-famous 'Obama.' It was a humorous way to connect with the historic figure who had captured the local's attention, even if only linguistically. Social media feeds were filled with funny banters implicating his name as 'Aboma'.

__A Fun Reminder:__ Just imagine what might have unfolded if Donald Trump had stumbled upon this playful twist on Barack Obama's name

during his first presidential campaign. It would have been a field day, adding another layer of intrigue to the already contentious "where is your birth certificate?" issue. Trump would have also asked proof of his real name. is it 'Aboma' from Ethiopia or Obama.

THE IDEA OF DONALD Trump, known for his outspoken and controversial statements, discovering this local linguistic playfulness could have led to an entertaining and possibly even more heated chapter in the political discourse of the time. It's almost as if this linguistic quirk, combined with the birther conspiracy theories, would have added yet another layer of intrigue to an already dramatic presidential campaign. For Ethiopians, we were interested in American politics and came up with our own way of naming and connecting as a gateway from our own complex and unrelatable politics that has no connection with its people. But, for Trump it would have been a fuel igniting his campaign; and thank God we are in Africa far separated from the rest of the world.

In what looks like a shared sentiment President Barack Obama became the first sitting US president to visit Ethiopia. He traveled to Addis Ababa, Ethiopia in late July 2015 to meet with the Ethiopian government and African Union leaders. I remember his visit to be unlike any other visits by a leader of a nation.

The city of Addis Ababa, the capital of Ethiopia hosts the African Union, the United Nations Economic Commission for Africa and countless numbers of Embassies prompting a frequent visit by heads of states from the entire Africa and the rest of the world. But, unlike any other visits the city has ever seen before that the arrival of Obama in the city was more than epic. There was American secret service arriving to the city with their own cars to transport the president. I have no idea whether that is customary everywhere they go but that was a first for a head of state to bring his own transportation for accompanying the convoy. It was a moment of show off no one really objected too, everyone knows how America is great and all so all the sentiment here was of admiration.

His visit though was nothing sort of a symbolic gesture giving legitimacy to one of the most repressive government in the African continent at that time characterized by forceful detention, killing and subjugation of journalists, politicians and the general public. It was a moment of heartbreak for politicians and human rights activists in the country missing such an opportunity from a person admired throughout the nation due to his charismatic messages of hope and democracy.

Geo-politically speaking Ethiopia has been a darling of American politicians throughout those repressive years of government the general public endured. These close relationship with Ethiopian government might have to do with the role Ethiopia has been playing in keeping security around the horn of Africa especially in Somalia fighting the Islamic extremist group Al Shabab. Due to these and other geo-political interest America has constantly poured in billions of dollars into Ethiopia while clearly understanding the repressive nature of the Ethiopian government during that period.

This might be the period I personally experienced and realized how great this nation thousands of miles away is. The Obama presidency by far was the pinnacle of democracy in me and my fellow citizens mind creating a clear sense of what America is made of. At this point in my discovery of America as a nation I realized the greatness of America lies within its people.

Chapter Ten: Late night comedy shows

"Late-night television isn't just about entertainment; it's a reflection of our society's humor, quirks, and concerns. It's where we gather to laugh at ourselves and find common ground."
- Johnny Carson

HUMOR, IN MANY WAYS, can serve as a powerful gateway to understanding a culture and its people. Even though, I cannot say the same for comics in my country while growing up, comedy in America looks like a reflection of a the coolest people on planet earth with a blasting unique perspectives on the world they live in. As far as I remember, Ethiopian comedians from the 90s and 2000s or 2010s were all into a slapstick comedy or some absurd skits that are regressive and unfunny with no content at all. So, there is a stark contrast between comedy I know and the comedy I was introduced to from American Television showing me a society wide apart from the one I know.

Especially, in the context of American politics, late-night TV hosts might have played a significant role in shaping public opinion and providing a platform for critical and humorous discourse for many across the US. Moreover, these TV geniuses have shaped philosophical and practical views of politics and society around the world in addition to their profound impact on my view about the United States of America. The liberal satirical take freely airing on national televisions across America and beyond made me appreciate the beauty of American democracy more and created a real representation of great nation in my mind. For someone who grew up in a political environment where people are thrown in prison for posting something funny about the ruling party or the government on social media, that was a dose of adrenaline rushing through my boring political life.

As far as my community is concerned politics is not up for comedy anywhere else. Be it social media or main stream media joking about governments or politics is not a norm at all. Social media sites blocking and being imprisoned for something someone said is very common.

There is an old saying in local language in Ethiopia which goes 'You can neither sue the government nor plough the sky'. The saying is a testament to the way we used to view governments here. Hence, speaking up against government is a taboo thing to do let alone have a funny banter about it on national television. Freedom of expression only exists within the confines of ones own home or room and that is it.

During Donald Trump's presidential campaign, I found myself gravitating towards late-night TV hosts who offered a unique, extremely funny, and unprecedented take on political humor. Their witty and often over the top satirical commentary provided a refreshing antidote to the American view I have personally developed over the years and my understanding of freedom of speech I was accustomed to.

I was particularly drawn to the way these hosts used humor to expose the absurdities of Trump's policies and behavior. The way they highlighted the hypocrisy, the incompetence, and the moral bankruptcy of his campaign plus his administration with a level of fun and stupidity that was unmatched by mainstream media outlets.

Well Fox news political commentators and journalists might have matched or even sometimes leaped the late-night comedy hosts in delivering funny and stupid take on politics of the US as far as comedy is concerned.

At some point in time, I realized the late-night comedy humor and the genius stupidity airing over the TV channels was not merely for entertainment purposes. It was more of a social commentary that challenged viewers to think critically about the political landscape and to hold their elected officials accountable in America while it was all fun and an earth-shattering change of perspective into what politics would look like in a free world for those of us outside of the United States. Late-night TV hosts became a remarkable source of insight into the American political psyche, offering a unique lens through which to navigate the complexities of America.

Trevor Noah, Stephen Colbert, John Oliver, James Corden, Jimmy Kimmel, Jimmy Fallon, and Samantha Bee: were some of the brilliant comedians and late-night hosts who collectively served as an incredible gateway to understanding America. With their witty commentary, irreverent humor, and sharp wit, they decoded the intricacies of

American life, offering a unique and invaluable window into the heart and soul of the nation.

More than mere entertainers, these late-night hosts became cultural interpreters, using humor as their language to bridge the gap between American values, ideals, and realities. They held a mirror to society, reflecting back its triumphs and failures, its hopes and fears, its contradictions and complexities. For individuals like me who were exposed to unrealistic depictions of American society throughout countless Hollywood movies this was a very important phenomenon.

Their humor was often biting, but it was always insightful. They poked fun at the powerful, challenged the status quo, and gave voice to the voiceless. They were not afraid to tackle difficult topics, from racism and sexism to political corruption and social injustice. It is may be those intricacies that made me realize and appreciate the amazing diversity this great nation boasts.

For me and countless others, these late-night hosts became more than just entertainers. They became educators, mentors, and perspective developers. They helped us to understand America from a very different viewpoint. It was a testament to the beauty of American freedom of speech that made me appreciate the US more and more as great nation.

Trevor Noah's incisive take on current events, Stephen Colbert's satirical wit, John Oliver's deep dives into complex issues, James Corden's playful charm, Jimmy Kimmel's heartfelt monologues, Jimmy Fallon's infectious humor, and Samantha Bee's fearless satire collectively offered a comprehensive, humorous, and sometimes even touching exploration of America.

There might be many more countless number of comedians out there in America hosting such shows but I am only exposed to those comedians I have seen on Youtube.

Through their comedic lens, these people turned complex topics into digestible and relatable anecdotes, making the often-baffling intricacies of American society feel accessible and comprehensible. They explored issues with a depth and nuance that was rarely found in mainstream media.

They were not afraid to tackle difficult and controversial subjects, and they often did so with a biting sense of humor. Their humor was not always easy to laugh at, but it was always thought-provoking. They forced us to confront the uncomfortable realities of American life and to examine our own biases and prejudices. In doing so, they played a vital role in shaping our viewpoints and perspectives about the definition of America as the nation.

The moment when President Trump appeared on Jimmy Fallon's show and was good-naturedly teased by the host was a moving reminder of the beauty of democracy for someone like me.

In a political campaign that that often looked divided and polarized, Fallon's interview with Trump served as a refreshing reminder that there is beauty in negating each other with ideas. It has also showcased the power of a good joke, even if it is at our own expense.

Fallon's decision to dress up as Trump and engage in a mirror interview was a stroke of comedic genius. It was a playful and irreverent take on the political process, yet it was also surprisingly insightful.

The mirror interview which I thought tried to force Trump to confront his own image, both literally and figuratively. It held him up to a mirror and showed him how he was perceived by the public in the United States. But, for me miles and miles away from the US soil it is a perfect representation of the freedom an individual can exercise in this great nation.

Late night comedy entirely created a positive complementary perspective about America in my mind. It was all about the sheer brilliance of this people and their entire government system working in the principles of democracy. And even making the very serious politics look that foolish in front of everyone by itself made me appreciate the American greatness.

It is important here to mention that American Late-night hosts in America made me hate local television shows and comedians to this date. Looking into the contents of the American shows the local comedians does not even look like amateur comedians. Even those who sometimes tried to copy the American shows and make some political jokes failed too hard since they do not have strong content, resorting to direct verbal assault of people.

In this stage of my life one thing is clear, that is the greatness of the American democracy and more than everything I came to know people in America can freely say whatever they want without any repercussion. This is a luxury no one affords in countries like Ethiopia let alone expressing it in a funny comedic way on national television.

Chapter Eleven: The Trump America and the Unmasking of the political Boogeyman in Ethiopia

"Donald Trump is a symptom of a larger problem in American politics, which is the rise of populism and nativism."
- Bernie Sanders, United States Senator

THE TRUMP ERA IN THE United States politics may well be one of the most unforgettable and remarkable periods in its history, especially for those of us who view it from the outside. Building on the momentum of the Obama presidency, the local media coverage surrounding the 2012 Trump election was nothing short of monumental here in Ethiopia. Unlike any other U.S. election, people across the country were glued to their seats from the very start, even during the primary elections.

Before that time, the concept of primaries was relatively unknown to many of us. However, the unique and extreme approach taken by Trump, which often made politics resemble a comedic show, captivated the attention of everyone, keeping them fixated on their TV screens during those days.

The vivid and often theatrical nature of Trump's campaign made politics accessible and engaging, even to those who had never been deeply involved in political discourse. It was a time when American politics felt more like a dramatic performance, drawing people in with its twists and turns. The unpredictability of it all became an irresistible magnet, compelling everyone to follow the unfolding story.

Across the vast expanse of Africa, politics is an arena reserved for the perpetually serious, those with faces etched in unwavering sternness, a trait they carry throughout their lives, from their youthful days to their final moments. It's a running joke among us Africans that if you're overly serious, politics is your calling. In our minds, politics is the domain of military figures – individuals who seem immune to the infectious laughter that follows a good joke, who remain stoic and unmoved by the rhythm of music, and who never appear to let their hair down and enjoy themselves, regardless of the situation. It's as if we've accepted that those who govern us must be devoid of the lightheartedness and joy that we, the ordinary citizens, allow ourselves to indulge in.

In the tapestry of my childhood memories, Ethiopian politicians stand out, not for their charisma or their ability to connect with the masses, but for their unwavering seriousness. Their faces were like chiseled stone, etched with a sternness that seemed to reflect a deep-seated discontent, as if they'd been carrying a lifelong grudge against the world. The idea of a 'people person', someone with a warm smile and an infectious laugh, navigating the political arena in Africa seems almost paradoxical, an oxymoron in a world where politicians are expected to maintain an air of unwavering seriousness. It's as if the weight of the nation's problems rests perpetually on their shoulders, demanding a constant display of seriousness and unwavering focus.

In the African political landscape, the concept of a 'people person' often takes on a different meaning, one that's less about charisma and more about the projection of power. Historically, the path to becoming a 'people person' in African politics has often been paved with displays of force and intimidation, a show of strength that commands respect, if not genuine affection.

The image of a stern-faced leader, unflinching in their resolve, meting out punishment and leading troops into battle, has long been the archetype of a 'people person' in African politics. This perception is deeply ingrained in our collective consciousness, shaping our expectations of those who aspire to govern us.

In this context, the idea of a comedian, a philanthropist, or a business magnate assuming political office seems almost absurd. A comic like Ukraine's Zelensky, with his ability to connect with the masses through humor and relatability, would be considered too lighthearted, too far removed from the perceived gravitas of African politics.

Similarly, a charitable figure like Mother Teresa, with her boundless compassion and selflessness, would be seen as too soft, too idealistic for the rough and tumble world of African politics. And a savvy businessperson like Warren Buffett, with his sharp mind and knack for navigating the complexities of the financial world, would be deemed too far away from politics.

These individuals, despite their remarkable achievements and unique talents, would likely be dismissed as unfit for the African political arena, their strengths seen as weaknesses in a system that values strength over empathy, seriousness over humor, and power over compassion.

Across the globe, politicians are often allegedly painted as masters of deceit, fluent in the language of lies and manipulation. In Ethiopia, this perception is no different except it is not allegedly and it is more of a reality. We've grown accustomed to the idea of politics as a shadowy game, where truth is often the first casualty, and promises are as ephemeral as the morning mist.

Against this backdrop, the transition from the inspirational Obama era to the Trumpian spectacle was a jarring shift for us Ethiopians in particular and Africans in general. It was like stepping out of a solemn symphony into a raucous carnival, a disorienting yet strangely captivating experience.

The Obama years had been a pure adrenaline rush of being represented and witnessing the power of democracy playout in front of us. His speeches resonated with an almost poetic rhythm, his words carefully chosen to inspire and uplift. In contrast, Trump's political ascent was a whirlwind of brash statements, unfiltered opinions, and audacious claims. It was like watching a reality show unfold on the political stage, a captivating blend of entertainment and disbelief.

For us Ethiopians, accustomed to the stern faces and measured tones of our own politicians, Trump's antics were a source of endless fascination. His unfiltered banter, his disregard for political correctness, and his fondness for self-glorification were a stark contrast to the carefully crafted personas of traditional politicians.

As Trump's campaign gained momentum, we watched with a mix of amusement and apprehension. His unconventional approach was a breath of fresh air, a break from the monotony of political rhetoric. Yet, there was an underlying sense of unease, a nagging feeling that this unpredictable figure could potentially disrupt the delicate balance of global politics.

Despite the reservations, there was an undeniable excitement surrounding Trump's candidacy. His brashness and bravado were a source of entertainment, a welcome distraction from the often-grim realities of our own political landscape. We rooted for him, not necessarily because we believed in his policies or his ability to lead, but because he represented a break from the norm, a chance to witness the spectacle of American politics unfold in a way we'd never seen before.

The Trump era was a period of unprecedented political theater, a time when the lines between reality and satire blurred into a dizzying spectacle. His unorthodox approach to politics was a source of endless fascination, particularly for those of us accustomed to the more traditional, somber style of political discourse.

Trump's penchant for misquoting or even inventing Bible verses, his self-proclaimed expertise in matters of faith, and his often-comical attempts to portray himself as a devout Christian provided a constant stream of amusement. It was as if he was playing a caricature of a politician, a larger-than-life figure who seemed to revel in defying expectations and breaking all the rules.

His linguistic creativity, his penchant for coining new words and phrases, often with questionable accuracy or relevance, added another layer to the Trumpian spectacle. His speeches were a linguistic roller coaster, a wild ride through a world where grammar and logic often took a backseat to hyperbole and self-glorification.

And then there were the jibes, the relentless stream of insults and verbal jabs directed at his opponents. Trump's sharp tongue spared no one, from political rivals to journalists to celebrities. His unfiltered remarks, often bordering on the offensive, were a source of both shock and amusement.

For us, watching from afar, the Trump era was a crash course in a totally new kind of American-style political entertainment. It was a period when politics shed its serious demeanor and embraced the absurd, a time when the world's most powerful nation turned its political stage into a reality show, with all its drama, unpredictability, and sheer entertainment value.

We witnessed how even the most serious business of human life, politics, could be transformed into a spectacle, a source of amusement and bewilderment. It was a stark contrast to our own political landscape, where seriousness and formality still reigned supreme.

The Trump era was a reminder that politics, like any human endeavor, is not immune to the forces of entertainment and spectacle.

The Trump era was a period of unprecedented global exposure for American politics. His flamboyant personality and unconventional approach to campaigning transformed political events into captivating spectacles, beamed across the world through a multitude of media channels.

In Ethiopia, the interest in American politics reached new heights during this time. The groundwork had been laid by the hugely popular Obama presidency, which had sparked a renewed fascination with the world's most powerful nation. When Trump emerged on the political scene, his larger-than-life persona and unconventional style captivated Ethiopian audiences.

Trump's primary debates, campaign rallies, and public appearances became must-watch events, broadcast on our television screens, radios, and mobile devices. The language barrier was no obstacle, as local media outlets provided translations and commentary, ensuring that every Ethiopian could follow the unfolding drama.

This interest in American politics wasn't driven by the usual factors that motivate international attention, such as vested national interests in business or political alliances. Instead, it was the sheer entertainment value, the thrill of witnessing the unpredictable spectacle of American politics, that drew us in.

Trump's antics were a source of endless fascination, his unfiltered remarks and outrageous claims providing a constant stream of amusement. It was like watching a reality show unfold on the global stage, with the most powerful nation in the world as the backdrop.

Trump's unconventional approach to politics, his willingness to break all the rules and defy expectations, turned the world's attention towards America, albeit for reasons that were not always flattering.

In the accounts of Ethiopian history, politics has often been a source of strife and division, a tumultuous arena where power struggles have played out, leaving deep scars on the nation's psyche. For generations, Ethiopians have witnessed the relentless cycle of conflict and instability, a seemingly endless succession of civil wars and power grabs that have left deep wounds on the collective consciousness.

Unlike nations that have enjoyed periods of relative political stability, Ethiopia's history has been marked by an almost perpetual state of flux. Even during those eras that might be considered relatively stable, there has always been an undercurrent of tension, a simmering discontent among various factions of society.

The roots of this instability can be traced to the very foundation of the Ethiopian state. The nation's history is a tapestry woven with tales of power struggles, of rulers who ascended to power through force, deceit, and terror, leaving a trail of resentment and division in their wake.

This pattern of forceful regime changes has been a recurring theme throughout Ethiopia's history. Over the past 150 years, a period relatively well documented and less susceptible to historical manipulation, the evidence is clear: the nation's rulers have repeatedly seized power through violence and intimidation, leaving a legacy of bitterness and distrust among the populace.

As a result, Ethiopians have developed a deep-seated wariness of politics, a sense of trepidation born from centuries of witnessing the destructive potential of political ambition. The very notion of a stable, peaceful political landscape seems almost mythical, a distant dream that has eluded the nation for far too long.

In the Ethiopian history, the concept of a peaceful political transition has been an elusive dream, a distant aspiration overshadowed by the harsh realities of conflict and division. The nation's political landscape has been a battleground, where the rise of one leader invariably ignites opposition from other factions, fueling a cycle of unrest and instability.

This pattern of political turmoil has deep roots in Ethiopia's social fabric, where ethnic and social divisions have often been exploited for political gain. The nation's rich diversity, a tapestry of cultures and traditions, has too often been used as a tool for division, pitting one group against another in the pursuit of power.

Against this backdrop of political upheaval, the fascination with American politics among Ethiopians takes on a deeper significance just for the entertainment value or the novelty of a different political system.

For many Ethiopians, politics has been a source of anxiety and fear, a taboo topic to be avoided at family gatherings and social events. The very mention of politics can trigger memories of past conflicts, of the deep-seated divisions that have plagued the nation for so long.

In my own family, politics was considered a forbidden subject. My parents discouraged any discussion about political matters, fearing it would lead to political participation by members of the family which might result in negative repercussion if that member takes the opposition political view against the ruling government. This aversion to political discourse was a reflection of the broader disconnect between politics and community in Ethiopia.

A poignant example of this disconnect was my mother's reaction to a dream she had about my younger brother just recently. She dreamt that he was visited by a prominent politician, a figure she recognized from television. The next morning, she called me, her voice filled with distress and concern. She feared that the dream was a portent of my brother's future involvement in politics, a prospect that filled her with dread. She pleaded with me to use my influence as his elder brother to steer him away from the treacherous path of politics.

We laughed about the incident later with him not with my mom though because I told her I have convinced him, but it underscored the deep-rooted fear and distrust associated with politics in Ethiopia. The fact that a dream could cause such distress speaks volumes about the disconnect between the political realm and the everyday lives of ordinary Ethiopians.

WITHIN THE HEART OF Ethiopia, a nation marked by a tumultuous political history, a curious paradox exists. Despite the frequent recurrence of civil wars, Ethiopia has managed to retain a sense of stability and strength, standing as a beacon of resilience amidst a region of fragile nations. This resilience, perhaps counterintuitively, may stem from the very disconnect between the ordinary people and the political realm.

Unlike the political apathy observed in some Western nations, where a sense of disillusionment or complacency has led to disengagement, the Ethiopian disinterest in politics is rooted in a deeper sentiment: fear. Politics, for many Ethiopians, is not a source of hope or empowerment, but rather a reminder of past conflicts, of the deep-seated divisions that have plagued the nation for so long. Politics has often been a zero-sum game, where the gains of one group come at the expense of another, perpetuating a cycle of instability and mistrust.

As a result, ordinary Ethiopians have developed a sense of self-preservation, a cautious detachment from the political arena. They focus on their daily lives, their families, and their communities, seeking solace and stability in the familiar rhythms of life, far removed from the volatile world of politics.

This detachment, while born out of fear, has paradoxically served as a stabilizing force. By distancing themselves from the political machinations, ordinary Ethiopians have, to some extent, shielded themselves from the destructive forces of political turmoil. They have preserved a sense of normalcy, a continuity of life that has enabled Ethiopia to weather the storms of political upheaval.

It's not that the public has never engaged in politics; there have been sporadic bursts of populist movements, moments when the masses rallied for change. However, these movements often ended in disappointment, their hopes dashed against the harsh realities of power struggles and unfulfilled promises.

This history of disillusionment has reinforced the perception of politics as a treacherous game, a realm where ordinary citizens have little chance of making a meaningful impact. Politics became the boogeyman, a cautionary tale that kept people at bay, wary of venturing into its treacherous depths.

Then came the Trump era, a whirlwind of unconventional political theatrics that shook the very foundations of American politics. Witnessing Trump's brash, unfiltered style, his willingness to challenge the establishment and break all the rules, was a revelation for many Ethiopians.

Here was a man who defied the traditional image of a politician. He spoke his mind, regardless of how outrageous or unconventional his statements might be. He attacked his opponents with schoolyard taunts and insults, seemingly impervious to the norms of political decorum.

For Ethiopians accustomed to a political landscape where fear and caution prevailed, Trump's antics were a breath of fresh air. It was as if the boogeyman had been exposed, revealing a more human, albeit flawed, face behind the mask of political power.

The realization that politics could be entertaining, even fun, was a paradigm shift for many Ethiopians. It challenged the deeply ingrained belief that politics was inherently a source of conflict and division.

However, for Ethiopians observing from afar, the Trump era offered a glimpse into a different kind of politics.

While the Trump era may have been a tumultuous chapter in American politics, it also served as a catalyst for Ethiopians to re-examine their own relationship with the political realm. It sparked a realization that politics doesn't have to be a source of fear and disillusionment, that it can be a space for engagement, debate, and even, at times, entertainment.

At this stage in my life America as a great nation with a cool tone started to make its way in my mind. I started to believe it is the only great nation that can make politics look and feel cooler.

Chapter twelve: The Trump America and the discovery of the heartland America

"Trump's election is a sign of the decline of American power and influence."
- Xi Jinping, President of China

AS THE POLITICAL LANDSCAPE of America unfolded on television screens across Ethiopia, a new perspective on the nation began to emerge. The intense coverage of the 2016 presidential election, with its focus on rallies, debates, and interviews with supporters of both Hillary Clinton and Donald Trump, revealed a side of America that was previously hidden from many Ethiopians.

The exposure to the heartland of America, to the voices of ordinary citizens from diverse backgrounds, shattered the stereotypical image of Americans as universally smart, intelligent, and extraordinary. It became apparent that, just like any other society, America had its share of individuals who lacked critical thinking skills or the ability to articulate their views in a coherent manner.

Witnessing these individuals expressing their opinions, sometimes in a manner that was both laughable and shameful, was a jarring experience for many Ethiopians. It challenged the idealized perception of America that had been shaped by Hollywood movies and popular culture.

However, this realization showed that Americans, despite their nation's global influence and technological advancements, were not immune to the same human flaws and imperfections that exist in every society. In a striking contrast to the viewpoints I developed over the years about America via different channels and meeting some two amazing ladies from the US, the people I witnessed giving interviews on Trump rallies proved to be a disappointment for me.

The 2016 election coverage, with its unfiltered exposure to the voices of ordinary Americans, served as a reminder that every society has its share of individuals who may not always express themselves in the most eloquent or informed manner. And this is before I even found out the worst ones to come after TikTok became a thing and exposed a wide variety of Americans naming Alaska and Texas among countries other than America. Or this was even way before finding out a majority of Americans considering the 54-nation continent of

Africa with hundreds of different ethnic groups as one single nation as Wakanda its capital city.

To make things more interesting, Donald Trump, a figure who defied all expectations, emerged as a bewildering anomaly in the American political landscape. His eccentricities and outlandish claims painted a stark contrast to the image of a shrewd, successful person I imagined to represent America.

As an outsider observing American culture, I had long held a certain reverence for the nation's intellectual prowess and its ability to produce exceptional individuals. However, Trump's ascent to political prominence shattered those idealized notions.

His peculiar mannerisms and unconventional vocabulary, including the infamous "covfefe" and "bigly," were a source of both amusement and embarrassment. His unwavering self-glorification, epitomized by his insistence on having "the best words," was both perplexing and cringeworthy even for me thousands of miles away in east Africa.

Trump's audacity extended beyond his linguistic inventions. He boldly asserted his biblical knowledge, yet his erroneous citations during rallies cast doubt on his grasp of the scriptures. These gaffes, coupled with his overall demeanor, made me question my long-held views about the US.

Beyond Trump's personal eccentricities, the unwavering support he received from individuals who identified as devout Christians was a source of deep consternation for me personally. Their endorsement of his behavior, often in the name of Christianity, challenged my understanding of how the faith was perceived in America.

As a devout Protestant Christian, I believe I have always held the exemplary life of Jesus as the cornerstone of my faith. Values such as humility, compassion, and forgiveness are central to my understanding of Christianity. Yet, Trump's actions, often characterized by cursing, divorce, intoxication, hate, and multiple marriages, seemed adversative to these principles I held dear to my heart for most of my life.

The uncritical acceptance and justification of these behaviors by some American Christians were perplexing and disheartening. It was as if they were willing to overlook these transgressions in favor of political allegiance. This disagreement between Trump's conduct and the core tenets of Christianity left me questioning the depth of their faith and their interpretation of biblical teachings. Further complicating my long held American greatness viewpoint by one group I thought I would have trusted with all my heart, the evangelicals. Evangelicals, are considered to be the epitome of biblical morality in my own community.

The unwavering support for Trump among certain Christian circles forced me to confront the reality that Christianity in America might be interpreted and practiced differently than I had always believed. It was a sobering realization that challenged my idealized perception of a perfect Christian community I personally believed in.

To clarify my position, I am not aligning myself with either the Democratic or liberal political factions here. In fact, I personally disagree with many of their championed ideologies. However, my exposure to political rallies and interviews transmitted via news channels and late night comedy shows led me to question the overall intellectual capacity of a significant portion of the American populace belonging highly to the republican or conservative faction.

The uncritical acceptance of misinformation, the prevalence of emotional rhetoric over rational discourse, and the widespread embrace of conspiracy theories have all contributed to this perception. These observations have raised concerns about the ability of a significant segment of the American public to engage in critical thinking and make informed decisions.

A very strange things like Trump's fixation on building a border wall and the fervent support it garnered from his base further eroded my idealized perception of American intellect. Interviews conducted at those rallies, in the heartland of America, revealed a stark reality: Americans, like my fellow Ethiopians, are a diverse mix of intelligence, ordinariness, brilliance, and folly.

In the never-ending number of cringeworthy strange incidents other things like Trump's obsession with his hands, his relentless attacks on Hillary Clinton, immigrants, and the media, all made me questions about the ethos of this supposedly great nation. His continuous "fake news" rants against the media, his demeaning "nasty woman" label for Hillary Clinton, and his sweeping generalization of Mexicans as "bad hombres" forced me to reevaluate my long held perception of America as a great nation with smart, intelligent and amazing people.

The America I had long admired, the land of opportunity, innovation, and intellectual prowess, seemed to be fading into a caricature of itself. The uncritical acceptance of Trump's divisive rhetoric and the enthusiastic applause it received from his supporters painted a disturbing picture of a nation intellectually compromised. Or just a nation faultily represented as the greatest among all countries in my mind as far as I am concerned.

So, this is a very important juncture that tested my unwavering view about the greatness of America with exposure to the ordinary Americans life.

Chapter thirteen: COVID 19 and The Trump Presidency

"It's going to disappear. One day, it's like a miracle, it will disappear."
- Donald Trump, February 27, 2020

WHILE MANY OF US HERE in Ethiopia initially found the American primaries entertaining, it was quite an unpleasant surprise when Donald Trump ultimately secured the presidency. Most Ethiopians, including myself, were drawn to the humor and often absurdity of American politics. We reveled in the sensationalism and the theatrical nature of it all. It was like a never-ending reality show that we watched from afar with both fascination and amusement.

However, none of us could have anticipated that Americans would elect a candidate who, in my opinion, fell far short of even basic standards of competence. The confusion that swept through our conversations was intense. We marveled at how a nation known for its technological advancements, scientific achievements, and global influence could endorse a leader who, to many of us, seemed remarkably ill-suited for the role. This sudden shift in our perception of America left us questioning the very foundations of our understanding of American politics and its influence on the world stage.

Bear in mind, my understanding of the American political landscape at that time was still in its early stages. The nuances of the American community, divided between Democrats and Republicans or liberals and conservatives, were yet to fully develop in my mind. To me, the election appeared to be a straightforward choice between two individuals, and I naively believed that the more intelligent candidate would emerge victorious.

My support for Hillary Clinton wasn't necessarily a personal endorsement, but rather an anticipation of witnessing a significant moment in American history. I envisioned that I would be a firsthand witness to the greatness of American democracy by experiencing the election of the first woman president, following the historic election of the first African American man who had become the first family of the United States of America. It was a perspective filled with hope and an expectation of greatness thrive.

For the majority of ordinary people in Ethiopia, the election was not about conservative versus liberal ideologies; it revolved around those two prominent candidates, Trump and Clinton. Their contrasting personas and policies drew the attention of the world, making it a global spectacle that transcended political intricacies. Little did we know how this choice would impact not only the United States but also countries far beyond its borders.

At that time, I was completely unaware of the underlying values and norms at play between these two individuals, Trump and Clinton. The intricacies of their differences eluded my understanding.

As a devout evangelical myself, I was astonished to discover that many American evangelicals were strong supporters of Trump. I had not expected evangelicals to rally behind a figure like Trump. In Ethiopia, the generation of evangelicals I was familiar with tended to be more educated and were often viewed as liberals and progressives in their outlook on the world. Our approach to faith was informed by a broader perspective, and we embraced a global view.

As a community considered somewhat of an "alien" religion within an Orthodox Christian majority, my perception of American evangelicals had always been influenced by a positive view. The idea of American evangelicals, whose values and beliefs were rooted in faith, had traditionally conveyed a sense of moral and ethical strength to me. It was a stark contrast to the political alignment I would later learn about, and it further underscored the complexity of American society and its diversity.

To my shock, Trump eventually secured the presidency, despite being marred by scandals, controversies, and a seemingly unending stream of negative headlines. It was a disconcerting time for me as an observer from afar.

The emergence of perplexing narratives, such as the notion of 'alternative facts,' championed by the Trump administration and its supporters, left me cringing. The blurring of truth and falsehood in public discourse in a country I considered to be the emblem of moral grounds and democracy was a cruel discovery.

Trump's childlike behavior, which often involved comparing himself to world leaders and attempting to elevate his own status above all others, made me seriously question my perception of America. It was as if the leader of one of the world's most influential nations was engaged in a playground game of one-upmanship.

One memorable instance that left me baffled to this date was Trump's tweet about the size of his nuclear button in comparison to North Korea's leader, Kim Jong Un. It oscillated between a source of headache and a moment of bemused laughter.

Trump's consistent use of the phrase like 'People are saying' always left me pondering the identity of these mysterious individuals who seemed to exclusively express unwavering admiration for him. It was a rhetorical device that added to the enigma of his presidency and my American viewpoint.

Collectively, these issues and similar incidents not only shattered my mythic view of America but also led me to question whether America's perceived greatness was a reflection of reality or merely a construct of the collective imagination.

To make matters even worse, in the year 2019, almost three years into the Trump presidency, the world was struck by the most devastating nightmare in recent memory: COVID-19. This global pandemic brought the entire world to a standstill, leaving us all in a state of shock and uncertainty.

At a time when the entire world was desperately searching for a savior and intelligent leadership, the scenes of hospitals overwhelmed by COVID-19 patients painted a grim picture. It was in this critical moment of human history that we found Donald Trump at the helm. The individuals who were once revered and expected to provide answers to the most pressing questions became the subject of jokes and skepticism (Courtesy of white-house COVID-19 briefings).

The world, grappling with an unprecedented crisis, found itself in a situation where leadership was vital, and intelligence was paramount. Instead, there was widespread disillusionment and a sense of disbelief as a leader known for his unconventional approach was tasked with navigating the greatest global challenge of our time and handled it like an amateur.

I still cringe when I remember the day Trump openly endorsed Hydroxychloroquine as a potential treatment for COVID-19, a stance that stood in stark contrast to the more cautious approach taken by professionals like Dr. Fauci. It was a puzzling and unsettling situation where the President of the United States openly advocated for a medication, while experts hesitated to endorse it fully.

To make matters even more bewildering and made my cringe even cringe, Trump suggested the injection of disinfectants as a potential treatment for the virus. This particular moment in his presidency made him appear, in the eyes of the world, like an uninformed child, completely out of touch with the reality of a being at the helm of the greatest nation on earth.

What struck me the most was the unwavering support he received from his followers, even when he made such outlandish remarks. Some segments of the media seemed to amplify his words without questioning, and this further eroded the mythical image I had held about America. It was a time when I questioned how such a phenomenon could occur in a nation I once believed to be the epitome of reason and rationality.

Moreover, I couldn't help but notice a growing trend of people claiming that COVID-19 was a hoax, echoing Trump's misinformation and alleging a 'deep state' conspiracy. It was a surreal moment when the boundaries between fact and fiction blurred, and the world witnessed the power of disinformation in the age of information spearheaded by the leader of the free world.

At a time when the world was eagerly looking for vaccines and hoping for a cure to emerge from the United States, our collective disappointment grew as we witnessed what seemed like a bad parody of a miracle on our TV screens. The anticipation for American leadership to shine through in the face of a global crisis was met with a feeling of inadequacy and confusion.

Amidst this chaos and global uncertainty, there came a day that would forever remain etched in the memory of every Ethiopian. It was the day when Trump, in the midst of international conversations, made a rather absurd comment about Ethiopia while discussing the Nile River with a foreign official.

The comment left many of us here in Ethiopia baffled, as it seemed to reflect a lack of understanding and perhaps even disrespect towards our nation. It was a stark reminder of the impact that American leadership and its words had on the world stage, for better or for worse.

For Ethiopians, the River Nile, fondly referred to as 'Abay River' in our homeland, holds a place of profound significance. 'Abay' is not just a geographical feature; it's a source of national pride that runs deep within the hearts of Ethiopians. In every corner of our lives, this mighty river weaves its way into our culture.

You can discover a rich tapestry of stories, songs, poems, idioms, folklores, and various art forms that revolve around the Abay River. It's not just a body of water; it's a symbol of our heritage and the embodiment of our identity.

Our connection to the river Abay is multi-dimensional. It's spiritual, as it has been a source of inspiration for generations. It's physical, as it sustains our land and provides the lifeblood for our agriculture. It's social, as it brings our communities together in celebration and reverence. And perhaps most importantly, it's emotional, as the Abay River is entwined with our sense of belonging and national pride.

Ethiopians take immense pride in being the source of the magnificent River Abay, which holds the distinction of being the longest river in the world. It's a testament to our country's natural beauty and our role as stewards of this majestic waterway.

For centuries, this mighty river has flowed from the highlands of Ethiopia, carrying its life-giving fertile soils downstream, nurturing the ancient civilizations of Egypt, while many Ethiopians continued to reside in poverty along its banks.

Around a decade ago, a profound sense of determination and purpose swept through Ethiopia. All Ethiopians, regardless of their circumstances, came together and pooled their resources to embark on the monumental task of constructing one of the largest hydroelectric dams on the Nile, known as the Abay River here. I recall the moment I contributed my very first paycheck as an employee, and it was a shared commitment echoed by countless others throughout Ethiopia. In essence, this dam represents the collective effort of a hundred million people, without exaggeration.

Now, you might be wondering what this has to do with America and the subject of this book about the United States. Let me explain.

America has maintained strong relationships with numerous African countries, including Ethiopia, for decades. However, when it comes to Africa, America's interest in one particular nation, Egypt, stands out. Egypt is a nation that has long regarded itself as the 'gift of the Nile.' It's worth noting that one could argue that Egypt's gifts are partially attributed to Ethiopia, and I can say to the world Egypt is actually 'A gift of Ethiopia' considering the constant flow of fertile soils and the uninterrupted water flow from the highlands of Ethiopia throughout known human history building everything Egypt is today or in the past.

Historically, only Sudan and Egypt have been the primary beneficiaries of the Abay River. This river, originating in Ethiopia, has played a pivotal role in shaping the livelihoods and destinies of these two nations, Egypt in particular. This creates a complex web of relationships, not just between African nations but also with external players like the United States, who have vested interests in the region.

With its deeply vested interest in the Nile, Egypt has consistently opposed the construction of the dam on the Abay River in Ethiopia from the very beginning. Egypt has employed a range of tactics and strategies to hinder Ethiopia's ambition to build the dam. These efforts have included sponsoring acts of terror, issuing direct threats of war, applying diplomatic pressure through channels like the United Nations, and leveraging international organizations.

The complex dynamics surrounding the construction of the dam not only reveal the depth of Egypt's concern over its share of Nile waters but also highlight the intricate geopolitical relationships in play.

Then came Trump, known for his unconventional diplomatic language. In 2019, then-President Donald Trump made a comment that was deemed by many as provocative and unorthodox. He suggested that Egypt had the capacity to "blow up" Ethiopia's Grand Ethiopian Renaissance Dam (GERD) on the Blue Nile River. This striking statement was made during a phone call with Sudanese Prime Minister Abdalla Hamdok, a conversation in which Trump was announcing the normalization of ties between Sudan and Israel.

Trump's diplomatic language and approach to this complex situation not only added a layer of tension to the existing dispute but also raised questions about the role of the United States in the region and its approach to such critical international matters. And more specifically deterred the mighty view about America in Ethiopia to nothing.

However, even though I eventually grasped that many within Trump's presidency didn't necessarily take his words at face value, the damage to my perception had already taken root. As the echoes of his unconventional statements reverberated across the world, they left a lasting impact on how I, along with many Ethiopians, viewed America. The mythic greatness of the United States, once firmly held in our collective imagination, began to shift into a more nuanced reality. We saw the United States not as an infallible paragon of virtue but as a nation populated by individuals of diverse backgrounds, from those with remarkable qualities to those with their own share of flaws.

The pivotal moment when this transformation in perception truly solidified was during the convergence of COVID-19 and Trump's presidency. It was then that the facade of unquestioned greatness started to crumble, unveiling a nation grappling with its own challenges and complexities. This awakening brought forth a realization that America, like any other nation, had its strengths and weaknesses, its moments of greatness, and its moments of vulnerability.

It was precisely at this juncture that I found myself contemplating the idea of writing this book. The experiences, the shifting dynamics, and the multifaceted nature of America as revealed during those challenging times became a powerful catalyst for exploring and understanding the intricate facets of this great nation.

Conclusion

America in my life is like a super hero I always admired and prolonged to imitate. But, it is a super hero that disappointed me as I grow older and became fully aware of the reality of the world around me. It is like transitioning from being amused by the Spider-Man movie perplexed by his jumping flexes to being amused by the behind the scenes video which made that amazing movie possible.

About the Author

Gemechu Birehanu Bekana Is a writer based In Addis Ababa Ethiopia with a decade experience in the higher education sector in Ethiopia. He can be contacted at gbekana13@gmail.com